Mediterranean Diet For Total Beginners

Amanda A. Noble

Introduction

This is a comprehensive guide that introduces you to the Mediterranean diet and helps you incorporate its principles into your lifestyle. The guide covers the basics of the Mediterranean diet, provides a 7-day meal plan, and offers a variety of energizing recipes for breakfast, lunch, dinner, snacks, and desserts. It also includes a quick nutritional reference table and a grocery list to make shopping easier.

The guide begins by explaining the Mediterranean diet and its health benefits. It emphasizes the consumption of whole foods, such as fruits, vegetables, whole grains, legumes, nuts, and olive oil, while limiting processed foods, red meat, and sugary beverages. It also highlights the importance of an energizing lifestyle, which includes regular physical activity, stress management, and social connections.

Next, the guide provides a 7-day meal plan to help you get started on the Mediterranean diet. It includes breakfast, lunch, dinner, and snack ideas for each day, making it easy to plan your meals and ensure a balanced diet.

For breakfast, you'll find energizing Mediterranean recipes that incorporate ingredients like fruits, whole grains, yogurt, and nuts. These recipes provide a nutritious and delicious way to start your day.

The guide also offers quick and easy Mediterranean lunch recipes, featuring salads, sandwiches, wraps, and soups. These recipes are designed to be simple yet flavorful, making them perfect for busy individuals.

When it comes to dinner, the guide presents sumptuous Mediterranean recipes that include a variety of vegetables, lean proteins, and healthy fats. These recipes showcase the vibrant flavors and culinary traditions of the Mediterranean region.

To satisfy your snack cravings, the guide provides easy Mediterranean snack recipes that are both nutritious and delicious. These recipes offer alternatives to processed snacks and highlight the use of fresh ingredients.

No meal is complete without dessert, and the guide includes heavenly Mediterranean dessert recipes that feature fruits, nuts, and traditional ingredients like honey and yogurt. These desserts offer a sweet ending to your Mediterranean meals.

For quick reference, a nutritional table is provided to help you understand the macronutrient composition of various foods commonly found in the Mediterranean diet.

Lastly, the guide offers a grocery list that serves as a handy tool when shopping for Mediterranean diet-friendly ingredients. It includes a variety of fruits, vegetables, whole grains, legumes, lean proteins, nuts, and olive oil.

Overall, this is a comprehensive guide that provides valuable information, meal plans, and recipes to help you embrace the Mediterranean diet and improve your overall well-being.

Contents

Most experts consider the traditional Mediterranean diet to be one of the healthiest in the world.

When you ponder about Mediterranean food, your mind perhaps flies off to pizza and pasta from Italy, or hummus and pita from Greece, but then again these dishes don't exactly suit into any healthy dietary plans promoted as "Mediterranean."

The truth is that a right Mediterranean diet comprises mainly of fruits and vegetables, seafood, olive oil, hearty grains, and additional foods that support the fight against heart disease, high blood pressure, highcholesterol, certain cancers, type-2 diabetes, and cognitive decline.

It's a diet worth pursuing; making the change from pepperoni and pasta to fish and avocados might take some effort, but you could before long be on your way to a healthier and longer life.

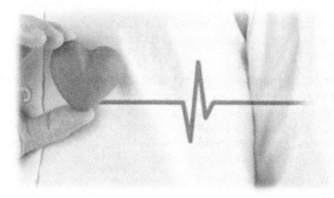

What is the Mediterranean Diet?

Pizza, gyros, falafel, lasagna, rack of lamb, and long loaves of white bread: all those foods have grown into synonymous with what we call "Mediterranean." We image giant, three-hour feasts with numerous courses and boundless bottles of wine. But over the last 50 years, Americans and others have changed the idea of Mediterranean fare, ramping up the calories and unhealthy fat at the cost of the region's traditional fruits, vegetables, beans, nuts, seafood, olive oil, dairy, and a glass or two of red wine.

What was formerly a healthy and inexpensive method of eating back then is now related with heavy, unhealthy dishes that contribute to heart disease, obesity, diabetes, mood disorders, and other health issues.

After World War II, a study directed by Ancel Keys of the Mayo Foundation studied the diets and health of nearly 13,000 middle-aged men in the US, Japan, Italy, Greece (including Crete), the Netherlands, Finland, and Yugoslavia. Strangely, well-fed American men had higher rates of heart disease than individuals in countries whose diets had been limited by the scarcities of war. It was the men of Crete, perhaps the poorer people of the study, who enjoyed the supreme cardiovascular health. This was due to physical work and their unique food pyramid.

The Mediterranean Diet Pyramid is founded on the eating traditions of Crete, Greece, and southern Italy around 1960 at a period when the rates of chronic disease among people were amongst the lowest in the world, and adult life probability was among the highest, even though medical services were restricted.

Aside from eating a diet containing mostly of fresh and homegrown foods instead of processed foods, other vital fundamentals to the Mediterranean diet are regular exercise, sharing meals with others, and nurturing a deep gratefulness for the pleasures of eating healthy and delicious foods.

Is the Mediterranean Diet for You?

Not only is the Mediterranean diet a tasty way to eat, drink and live, but it's also a realistic and sustainable way to reduce disease-causing inflammation and lose weight, too (or maintain a healthy weight).

The Mediterranean diet has long been one of the healthiest diets known to man. But it's not just a diet or even a way of eating … it's really a way of life. Because for thousands of years people living along the Mediterranean coast have indulged in a high-fiber diet of fruits and vegetables, also including quality fats and proteins and sometimes a glass of locally made wine to complete a meal, too. Meanwhile, this diet has gotten a reputation for disease prevention and even "enjoyable" weight management.

If you are still questioning if this diet is for you let me show you eight of the most valuable benefits of the Mediterranean Diet:

1. Low in Processed Foods and Sugar

The diet primarily comprises of foods and ingredients that are very close to nature, containing olive oil, legumes like peas and beans, fruits, vegetables, unrefined cereal products, and small percentages of animal products (that are always "organic" and locally produced). In contrast to the usual American diet, it's very low in sugar and basically free of all GMOs or artificial ingredients like high fructose corn syrup, preservatives and flavor enhancers. For a touch sweet, people in the Mediterranean enjoy fruit or small amounts of homemade desserts prepared with natural sweeteners like honey.

Beyond plant foods, the additional major staple of the diet is locally caught fish and a moderate consumption of cow, goat or sheep cheeses and yogurts that are incorporated as a way to get healthy fats and cholesterol. Fish like sardines and anchovies are an essential part of the diet, which generally is traditionally lower in meat products than various Western diets today.

While most people in the Mediterranean aren't vegetarians, the diet encourages only a small consumption on meats and heftier meals — instead going for the lighter and healthier fish choices across the board. This can be beneficial for those considering to lose weight and improve things such as their cholesterol, heart health and omega-3 fatty acid intake.

2. Helps You Lose Weight in Healthy Way

If you're considering to lose weight without being hungry and maintain that weight in a realistic way that can last a lifetime, this might be the plan for you. The diet is both maintainable and worthwhile, and has been take on by countless people all over the world with great success related to weight loss and more, as it works to help manage weight and decrease fat intake naturally and effortlessly due to eating various nutrient-dense foods.

There's room for interpretation in the Mediterranean diet, whether you favor eating lower-carb, lower-protein or someplace in between. The diet focuses on eating healthy fats while keeping carbohydrates fairly low and improving a person's intake of high-quality proteins. If you prefer protein over legumes and grains, you have the opportunity to lose weight in a healthy, no-deprivation-kind-of-way with a high amount of seafood and quality dairy products (that instantaneously deliver other benefits like omega-3s and often probiotics).

Fish, dairy products, and grass-fed/free-range meats have healthy fatty acids that the body needs, working to help you feel full, manage weight gain, regulate blood sugar, and improve your mood and energy levels. But if you're more of a plant-based consumer, legumes and whole grains (especially if they're soaked and sprouted) also make good, filling choices.

3. Improves Heart Health

The study shows that bigger adherence to the traditional Mediterranean diet, containing plenty of monounsaturated fats and omega-3 foods, is linked with a significant decrease in all-cause mortality, particularly heart disease. A remarkable protective effect of a Mediterranean diet rich in alpha-linolenic acid (ALA) from olive oil has been displayed in many studies, with some finding that a Mediterranean-style diet can reduce the risk of cardiac death by 30 percent and sudden cardiac death by 45 percent.

A study from the Warwick Medical School also illustrates that when high blood pressure is compared to people consuming more sunflower oil and those consuming more extra-virgin olive oil, the olive oil decreases blood pressure by significantly greater amounts.

Olive oil is furthermore beneficial for lowering hypertension since it makes nitric oxide more bio available, which makes it better able to keep arteries dilated and clear. One more protective element is that it helps fight the disease-promoting effects of oxidation and improves endothelial function. Keep in mind that low cholesterol levels are not as good as high sometimes, but people in the Mediterranean don't generally struggle to maintain healthy cholesterol levels either since they get plenty of healthy fats.

4. Helps Fight Cancer

According to the *European Journal of Cancer Prevention*, "The biological mechanisms for cancer prevention associated with the Mediterranean diet have been related to the favorable effect of a balanced ratio of omega-6 and omega-3 essential fatty acids and high amounts of fiber, antioxidants and polyphenols found in fruit, vegetables, olive oil and wine."

Plant foods, particularly fruits and vegetables, are the cornerstone of the Mediterranean diet, which fight cancer in almost every way — providing antioxidants, guarding DNA against damage, preventing cell mutation, lowering inflammation and suspending tumor growth. Many studies point to the fact that olive oil might furthermore be a natural cancer cure and decrease the risk of colon and bowel cancers. It might have a protective effect on the growth of cancer cells due to lowered inflammation and reduced oxidative stress, plus its tendency to stimulate balanced blood sugar and a healthier weight.

5. Prevents or Treats Diabetes

Evidence suggests that the Mediterranean diet aids as an anti-inflammatory dietary pattern, which could help fight diseases connected to chronic inflammation, together with metabolic syndrome and type 2 diabetes. One reason the Mediterranean diet might potentially be so beneficial for preventing diabetes is because it controls surplus insulin, a hormone that controls blood sugar levels, makes us gain weight and keeps the weight on despite us dieting.

By regulating blood sugar levels with a balance of whole foods — having healthy fatty acids, quality sources of protein and some carbohydrates that are low in sugar — the body burns fat more proficiently and has more energy too. *A low-sugar diet with plenty of fresh produce and fats is a natural diabetes cure.*

According to the American Heart Association, the Mediterranean diet is higher in fat than the standard American diet, yet lower in saturated fat. It's approximately a ratio of *40 percent complex carbohydrates, 30 percent to 40 percent healthy fats and 20 percent to 30 percent quality protein foods.* Because this balance is to some degree ideal in terms of keeping weight gain and hunger under control, it's a good way for the body to stay in hormonal homeostasis, so somebody's insulin levels are return to normal. As a side effect, it also means someone's mood is more likely to stay positive and relaxed, energy levels up, and physical activity easier.

The Mediterranean diet is low in sugar, as the only sugar present typically comes from fruit, wine and the occasional locally prepared dessert. When it comes to drinks, lots of people drink good deal of fresh water, some coffee and red wine, too. But soda and sweetened drinks aren't nearly as common as they are in the U.S.

While few Mediterranean diets do contain a good deal of carbohydrates — in the form of pasta or bread, for example — being active and otherwise consuming very low levels of

4

sugar means that insulin resistance stays rare in these countries. The Mediterranean style of eating helps prevent peaks and valleys in blood sugar levels, which kills energy and takes a toll on your mood. All of these different factors contribute to this diet's diabetes prevention capabilities.

6. Protects Cognitive Health and Can Improve Your Mood

Eating the Mediterranean way may be a natural Parkinson's disease treatment, a great way to safeguard your memory, and a step in the right direction for naturally treating Alzheimer's disease and dementia. Cognitive disorders can happen when the brain isn't receiving an adequate amount of dopamine, an essential chemical required for proper body movements, mood regulation and thought processing.

Healthy fats like olive oil and nuts, plus plenty of anti-inflammatory veggies and fruits, are well-known to fight age-related cognitive decline. These help counter the damaging effects of exposure to toxicity, free radicals, inflammation-causing bad diets or food allergies, which can all add to impaired brain function. This is one reason why adherence to the Mediterranean diet is related with lower rates of Alzheimer's.

Probiotic foods like yogurt and kefir as well help form a healthy gut, which we now know is tied to cognitive function, memory and mood disorders.

7. Might Help You Live Longer!

A diet high in fresh plant foods and healthy fats looks to be the winning combination for longevity. Monounsaturated fat, the kind found in olive oil and some nuts, is the central fat source in the Mediterranean diet. Over and over, studies indicate that monounsaturated fat is linked with lower levels of heart disease, cancer, depression, cognitive decline and Alzheimer's disease, inflammatory diseases, and more. These are at this time the leading causes of death in developed countries — especially heart disease.

In the well-known Lyon Diet Heart Study, people who had heart attacks between 1988 and 1992 were either encouraged to follow the standard post-heart attack diet advice, which reduces saturated fat hugely or advised to follow a Mediterranean style. After roughly four years, follow-up results indicated that people on the Mediterranean diet experienced 70 percent less heart disease — which is about three times the decrease in risk accomplished by most cholesterol-lowering prescription drugs! The people on the Mediterranean diet also astonishingly experienced a 45 percent lower risk of all-cause death than the group on the usual low-fat diet.

These results were correct even though there wasn't much of a change in cholesterol levels, which conveys you that heart disease is about more than just cholesterol. The results of the Lyon Study were so remarkable and groundbreaking that the study had to be ended early for ethical reasons, so all participants could do the higher-fat Mediterranean-style diet and reap its longevity-promoting benefits.

8. Helps You De-stress and Relax

One more prompting factor is that this diet inspires people to spend time in nature, get good sleep and come together to connect over a home-cooked healthy meal, which are great ways to eliminate stress and, therefore, help stop inflammation. Commonly, people in these regions make sure to devote a lot of time outdoors in nature; eating food surrounded by family and friends (rather than alone or on-the-go); and find time to laugh, dance, garden and practice hobbies.

We all know that chronic stress can destroy your quality of life alongside with your weight and health. Those who practice the diet have the luxury of restful dining at a slow pace, eating local enjoyable foods almost every day and engaging in regular physical activity too — other essential factors that help uphold a happy mood.

In addition, the history of the Mediterranean diet includes a love for and captivation with wine — mainly red wine, which is considered beneficial and protective in moderation. For instance, red wine can help fight obesity, among other benefits. This nifty choice of a healthy way of life leads to longer lives liberated of chronic problems and diseases connected to stress, such as those caused by hormonal imbalances, fatigue, inflammation and weight gain.

Mediterranean Diet Food Pyramid Explained

These days the Mediterranean Diet is more popular than ever, with new studies every month supporting its benefits.

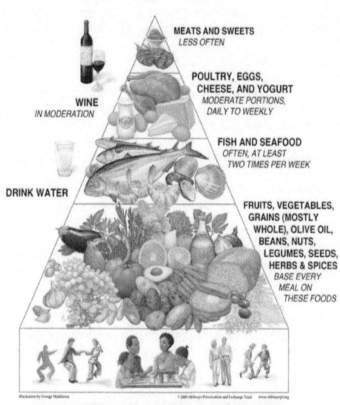

Beginning at the base of the pyramid, you'll find a huge priority on activity and social connections. Going up, you'll see the primary foods that you'll shop for and enjoy every day: whole grains, fruits, vegetables, beans, herbs, spices, nuts and healthy fats such as olive oil. Fish and seafood are normally eaten at least twice a week, and dairy foods – particularly fermented dairy like yogurt and traditional cheese – are eaten frequently in moderate portions. Eggs and occasional poultry are also part of the Mediterranean Diet, but red meat and sweets are not often eaten. Water, and wine (for those who drink) are usual beverages.

which is important for overall good health, includes strenuous exercise such as running and aerobics, more leisurely activities such as walking and house-or-yard work, and simple changes, such as taking the stairs instead of the elevator. Add physical activity to each day.

FRUITS, VEGETABLES, GRAINS (MOSTLY WHOLE), OLIVE OIL, BEANS, NUTS, LEGUMES, SEEDS, HERBS & SPICES,

represent the core of the diet. Base every meal on them. Olive oil, the main source of dietary fat, is used for almost all cooking and baking, and for dressing salads and vegetables.

FISH AND SEAFOOD

occupy their own section, since they are important sources of protein. Fish such as tuna, herring, salmon, and sardines are rich in heart-healthy omega-3 fatty acids, and shellfish including mussels, oysters, shrimp, and clams have similar benefits. Enjoy at least twice a week.

POULTRY, EGGS, CHEESE & YOGURT

form a central part of the Mediterranean Diet and are eaten in moderate portion sizes several times a week. Cheese, for example, is eaten regularly but in small amounts.

MEATS AND SWEETS

these are "sometimes" foods to eat less often. If you eat meat, choose small portions of lean cuts, such as round, shoulder, tenderloin, strip, T-bone, and flank. Enjoy sweets at a celebration or as a treat.

WINE AND WATER

wine can be consumed regularly but moderately: up to one glass per day for women, two for men. Water is essential for proper hydration, and contributes to health, well-being, and energy.

Common Foods and Flavors of the Mediterranean Diet Pyramid

1. Vegetables & Tubers

Artichokes, Arugula, Beets, Broccoli, Brussels, Spouts, Cabbage, Carrots, Celery, Celeriac, Chicory, Collard Cucumber, Dandelion Greens, Eggplant, Fennel, Kale, Leeks, Lemons, Lettuce, Mache, Mushrooms, Mustard Greens, Nettles, Okra, Onions (red, sweet, white), Peas, Peppers, Potatoes, Pumpkin, Purslane, Radishes, Rutabega, Scallions, Shallots, Spinach, Sweet Potatoes, Turnips, Zucchini

2. Fruits

Avocados, Apples, Apricots, Cherries, Clementines, Dates, Figs, Grapefruit, Grapes, Oranges, Melons, Nectarines, Olives, Peaches, Pears, Potatoes, Pomegranates, Strawberries, Tangerines, Tomatoes

3. Grains

Breads, Barley, Buckwheat, Bulgur, Couscous, Durum, Farro, Millet, Oats, Polenta, Rice, Wheatberries

4. Fish & Seafood

Abalone, Cockles, Clams, Crab, Eel, Flounder, Lobster, Mackerel, Mussels, Octopus, Oyster, Salmon, Sardines, Sea Bass, Shrimp, Squid, Tilapia, Tuna, Whelk, Yellowtail

5. Poultry, Eggs, Cheese & Yogurt

Chicken, Duck, Guinea Fowl

Eggs (Chicken, Quail, and Duck)

Cheese (Examples include: Brie, Chevre, Corvo, Feta, Haloumi, Manchego, Parmigiano-Reggiano, Pecorino, Ricotta)

Yogurt, Greek Yogurt

6. Nuts, Seeds & Legumes

Almonds, Beans (Cannellini, Chickpeas, Fava, Kidney, Green), Cashews, Hazelnuts, Lentils, Pine Nuts, Pistachios, Sesame Seeds (Tahini), Split Peas, Walnuts

7. Herbs & Spices

Anise, Basil, Bay Leaf, Chiles, Clove, Cumin, Fennel, Garlic, Lavender, Marjoram, Mint, Oregano, Parsley, Pepper, Pul Biber, Rosemary, Sage, Savory, Sumac, Tarragon, Thyme, Zatar

8. Meats & Sweets

Pork, Beef, Lamb, Mutton, Goat

Sweets (Example include: Baklava, Biscotti, Crème Caramel, Chocolate, Gelato, Fruit Tarts, Kunefe, Lokum, Mousse Au Chocolat, Sorbet, Tiramisu)

9. Water & Wine

Drink Plenty of Water

Wine in Moderation

A Mediterranean lifestyle embraces much more than just red wine and olive oil; physical activity and social connection are vital as well. To this point, researchers monitored 11,800 Spanish adults for 8.5 years observing their eating patterns, lifestyle, and health results.

Those most faithfully following a Mediterranean Diet were 18% less likely to cultivate depression over the 8.5-year study. Likewise, those with the most physical activity and social activity were 19% and 23% less likely to cultivate depression.

However, a Mediterranean lifestyle, which embraces diet, physical activity, and social activity, appeared to be most effective, as it was connected with a 50% lower risk of depression.
Clinical Psychological Science. 2016 Nov. 4(6):1085-10093. (Sanchez-Villegas A et al.)

How to Lose Weight on the Mediterranean Diet

Weight loss is significant issue for many people (and perhaps you) in the world nowadays. You may be searching for a way to shed some weight and think that the Mediterranean diet is the way to go. Selecting a Mediterranean diet isn't going to be a traditional "diet" or a quick fix.

Rather, it's a small steps of healthy lifestyle choices that can get you to your weight loss goal while you eat delicious, appetizing foods and get out and enjoy life. Sounds much better than counting calories and depriving yourself, right?

With that picture in mind, you need to focus on a small number of must-haves with the Mediterranean lifestyle in order to lose weight successfully. You have to pay attention to lifestyle changes, manage your calorie intake through balancing food choices and controlling portions, and increase your physical activity.

Here's are the steps on how to do this:

Step 1. Focus On Lifestyle Changes

The attention of the Mediterranean diet is on your whole lifestyle. Paying attention to lifestyle changes, such as changing your portion sizes and physical exercise regularly, is the only way to see long-term results. Weight-loss diets come and go, and most can help you lose the weight, but they aren't something you can live with long term.

The Mediterranean diet helps you pay attention to your individual lifestyle, including the types of foods you consume, the portion sizes you eat, your physical activities, and your whole way of life. You can fit in these changes into your daily life and create long-term routines that bring you not only weight loss but also sustained weight loss.

Set realistic, practical, and measurable goals.

Quit diets once and for all.

Make time in a fast-paced lifestyle.

When incorporating the Mediterranean diet into your lifestyle, your first goal is to try to slow down. Look at all you have on your (figurative) plate and see whether you can start to say "no" to some things so you can free up time for yourself.

Create small changes that stick.

Look at small goals you can integrate into your daily life and do it.

Step 2. Consider Calories without Counting Them

Calories are one of the most important concepts of weight loss. Basically, calories are the amount of energy in the foods you eat and the amount of energy your body uses for daily activities. Your body constantly needs energy or fuel not only for daily activities such as cooking, cleaning, and exercising but also for basic biological functions (like, you know, breathing).

Everyone has a different metabolic rate that determines how quickly he or she burns calories and depends on factors such as age, genetics, gender, and physical fitness level.

At the end of the day, you can't lose weight if you eat more calories than you burn through daily activity and exercise. To lose weight, you have to create a calorie deficit, but you can do so without actually knowing how many calories you burn. All you have to do is make small changes to your lifestyle, such as reducing portion sizes and exercising more, to reduce your calorie intake.

Eat more to lose weight.

Unlike many weight-loss diets, a Mediterranean style of eating lets you have more food on your plate while still taking in fewer calories. Eat far more low-calorie vegetables and fewer high-calorie meats and grains. As an added bonus, these lower-calorie foods also help you feel more satisfied with your meal instead of feeling deprived.

Take portion size into account.

Paying attention to portion sizes is a far better way to decrease your calorie intake than counting calories. Portion sizes in the Mediterranean are different than they are in the United States, which is one reason folks in the Mediterranean region tend to manage their weights more effectively.

Watch your fat calories.

The Mediterranean diet also allows you to keep track of the calories you get from fat. Although people on the Mediterranean coast eat slightly more fat than is recommended in the United States (35 percent of their calories come from fat, versus the U.S. recommendation of 30 percent), they consume different types of fat, such as the healthy fats from olive oil.

Increase the activity you love.

Exercise is an important component to weight loss and health, especially with the Mediterranean diet. You have to use up some of your calorie intake as energy, or those calories will store as fat. Exercise allows you to not only burn calories but also strengthen your heart, manage stress, and increase your energy level.

Step 3. Suppress Your Appetite

Eating a Mediterranean style diet is not only great for your health but can also work as a natural appetite suppressant to help manage your weight. When you eat the right balance of plant-based foods and healthy fats, your body works in a natural way to feel satisfied. Because you're full, you're not tempted (at least, not by your stomach) to snack on high-calorie junk food a short while after your last meal.

> Load up on fiber.
>
> Turn on your fullness hormones.

The Mediterranean diet is naturally high in low-glycemic foods, those carbohydrate-containing foods that illicit a lower blood sugar spike. Low-glycemic foods may just help kick on your fullness response. Appetite is controlled by an intricate dance of hormones that trigger the feelings of hunger and fullness.

Food cravings occur for many reasons, whether they're physiological, psychological, or a combination of both. For instance, having a stressful day at work may lead to food cravings. Unfortunately, no one-size-fits-all-answer exists to deal with food cravings, but you can do a few things to manage them more effectively.

> Avoid blood sugar spikes.
>
> Make sure you don't skip meals or wait longer than 5 hours to eat. Eat a meal or snack every 3 to 5 hours. Eat when you are hungry instead of waiting until you have extreme hunger.
>
> Eat protein-rich foods and a bit of fat. Include foods such as fish, beans, nuts, or eggs with a fat with each meal to help slow down your digestion
>
> Eat high-fiber, fruits, vegetables, grains, and legumes with each meal and snack. You don't have to eat these foods all at once, but including some combination of them at meals and incorporating a fruit, veggie, or whole grain with your snacks is a good idea.
>
> Manage your stress hormones.

You can accomplish this by exercising, getting enough sleep, drinking water, practicing deep breathing, meditating, and relaxing. For example, if you are getting ready for a stressful meeting, take a few moments to do some deep breathing. Simply take a deep breath, hold it for a few seconds, and let the air out. Keep repeating for as long as you can. Even a few minutes can help.

Hydration and You: Why it's So Important

Your body depends on water to survive. Every cell, tissue, and organ in your body needs water to work correctly. For example, your body uses water to maintain its temperature, remove waste, and lubricate joints. Water is needed for good health.

Symptoms of dehydration include the following:

> Little or no urine, or urine that is darker than usual
> Dry mouth
> Sleepiness or fatigue
> Extreme thirst
> Headache
> Confusion
> Dizziness or lightheaded feeling
> No tears when crying

Don't wait until you notice symptoms of dehydration to take action. Actively prevent dehydration by drinking plenty of water.

You may need to increase the amount of water you are drinking if you:

> Have certain medical conditions, such as kidney stones or bladder infection
> Are pregnant or breastfeeding
> Will be outside during hot weather
> Will be exercising
> Have a fever
> Have been vomiting or have diarrhea
> Are trying to lose weight

How muchwater should I drink each day?

You may have heard different recommendations for daily water intake. Most people have been told they should drink 6 to 8 8-ounce glasses of water each day, which is a reasonable goal. However, different people need different amounts of water to stay hydrated.

Most healthy people can stay well hydrated by drinking water and other fluids whenever they feel thirsty. For some people, fewer than 8 glasses may be enough. Other people may need more than 8 glasses each day.

If you are concerned that you are not drinking enough water, check your urine. If your urine is consistently colorless or light yellow, you are most likely staying well hydrated. Dark yellow or amber-colored urine is a sign of dehydration.

Tips for staying hydrated

Keep a bottle of water with you during the day. Purchasing bottled water is expensive and creates plastic bottle waste. Carry a reusable water bottle and fill it from the tap instead.

If you don't like the taste of plain water, try adding a slice of lemon or lime to your drink.

Be sure to drink water before, during, and after a workout.

When you're feeling hungry, drink water. Thirst is often confused with hunger. True hunger will not be satisfied by drinking water. Drinking water may also contribute to a healthy weight-loss plan. Some research suggests that drinking water can help you feel full.

If you have trouble remembering to drink water, drink on a schedule. For example, drink water when you wake up; at breakfast, lunch, and dinner; and when you go to bed. Or drink a small glass of water at the beginning of each hour.

Drink water when you go to a restaurant. It will keep you hydrated, and it's free!

QUICK & EASY 7-DAY MEAL PLAN

In this section, you will find Mediterranean breakfast menu and Mediterranean diet snack ideas for a whole week. And of course, Mediterranean lunch, dessert and diet dinner ideas.

Feel free to change recipe suggestions in the 7-Day Meal Plan.
Choose those you find work best for you.

Monday		
Breakfast	Mediterranean Breakfast Quinoa	28
Snack	Crispy Lentil Energy Bites	111
Lunch	Hearty Salmon Quinoa Burgers	61
Snack	Portobello Mushroom Delight	114
Dinner	Tilapia Al Ajillo	94

Tuesday		
Breakfast	Mediterranean Breakfast Quinoa	28
Snack	Crispy Lentil Energy Bites	111
Lunch	Yummy Tuna	55
Snack	Tomato-Basil Skewers	120
Dinner	Savory Lemon	95

Wednesday		
Breakfast	Mediterranean Breakfast Quinoa	28
Dessert	Caramel Apple Fluff	127
Lunch	Pork Tenderloin Apricot Salad	83
Snack	Hardboiled Egg and Avocado Bowl	117
Dinner	Chicken with Lemon	102

Thursday		
Breakfast	Pumpkin Oatmeal	35
Snack	Zesty Black Bean Hummus	112
Lunch	Yummy Tuna	55
Snack	Hardboiled Egg and Avocado Bowl	117
Dinner	Savory Lemon	95

Friday		
Breakfast	Pumpkin Oatmeal	35
Snack	Zesty Black Bean Hummus	112
Lunch	Chicken Salad with Grapes	69
Snack	Portobello Mushroom Delight	114
Dinner	Chicken with Lemon	102

Saturday		
Breakfast	Pumpkin Oatmeal	35
Snack	Greek Peanut Butter Yogurt	115
Lunch	Turkey Lettuce Wraps	76
Snack	Portobello Mushroom Delight	114
Dinner	Appetizing Tuna	85

Sunday		
Breakfast	Hearty Apple Almond Oatmeal	37
Dessert	Greek Baklava	121
Lunch	Turkey Lettuce Wraps	76
Snack	Tomato-Basil Skewers	120
Dinner	Appetizing Tuna	85

PART TWO
ENERGIZING MEDITERRANEAN
BREAKFAST RECIPES

The Mediterranean diet is widely known for using a wide array of lean protein, complex carbohydrates and healthy fats in just about any meal. And the most important meal of the day is no exception.

Choose and enjoy any one of these invigorating breakfast treats early in the morning and get a dose of energy without the unhealthy food cravings afterward.

MEDITERRANEAN BREAKFAST QUINOA

Serves 4 / Prep time: 10 min / Cook time: 15 min / Total Time: 25 min

Ingredients:

1/4 cup chopped raw almonds

1 cup quinoa

1 tsp. ground ground cinnamon

1 tsp. sea salt

2 cups milk

1 tsp. vanilla extract

2 tbsp. honey

2 dried pitted dates, finely chopped

5 dried apricots, finely chopped

Directions:

1   Over medium heat toast the almonds in a skillet until just golden, 3 – 5 minutes. Set aside when done.

2   Heat in a saucepan, together, quinoa and ground cinnamon over medium heat until warmed through.

3   In the saucepan add sea salt and milk and start stirring. Bring the mix to a boil, decrease the heat to low, put a cover on the saucepan and let it cook at a simmer for 15 minutes.

4   Into the quinoa mixture stir the vanilla, dates, honey, apricots and around half the almonds. Use the remaining almonds on the top. *Enjoy!*

PER SERVING - Calories: 327kcal; Fat:7.9g; Saturated fat:1.8g; Cholesterol:10mg; Carbohydrate:53.9g; Sugar:24.1g; Fiber:5.8g; Protein:11.5g

FRESH BLACKBERRIES QUINOA

Serves 2 / Prep time: 10 min / Cook time: 10 min / Total Time: 20 min

Ingredients:

1/2 cup quinoa	1/2 tsp. vanilla extract
1/2 cup water	1/2 cup dried cherries
1/2 cup skim milk	1 tablespoon honey
1/2 tsp. ground cinnamon	1/2 cup fresh blackberries

Directions:

1   Bring quinoa, water, milk, cinnamon, and vanilla extract to a boil in a saucepan.

2   Reduce heat to medium-low, cover, and simmer until quinoa is tender and has absorbed the water, 10 to 15 minutes. Remove saucepan from heat.

3   Mix cherries, cashews, and honey into the quinoa mixture. Top with blackberries. *Enjoy!*

PER SERVING - Calories: 597kcal; Fat:24.3g; Saturated fat:7g; Cholesterol:22mg; Carbohydrate:80.7g; Sugar:32.7g; Fiber:9.1g; Protein:16.4g

QUINOA BREAKFAST BOWL

Serves 2 / Prep time: 5 min / Cook time: 20 min / Total Time: 25 min

Ingredients:

1/2 cup water

1/4 cup red quinoa

1 1/2 tbsp. extra-virgin olive oil

2 eggs

1 pinch salt and ground black pepper to taste

1/4 tsp. seasoned salt

1/4 tsp. ground black pepper

1 avocado, diced

2 tablespoons crumbled feta cheese

Directions:

1   Stir water and quinoa together in a rice cooker. Cook until quinoa is tender, about 15 minutes.

2   Heat olive oil in a skillet over medium heat and cook eggs to desired doneness; season with seasoned salt and pepper.

3   Combine quinoa and eggs in a bowl; top with avocado and feta cheese. *Enjoy!*

PER SERVING - Calories:372; Fat:26.8g; Saturated fat:5.6g; Cholesterol:194mg; Carbohydrate:24.1g Sugar:1.4g; Fiber:8.8g; Protein:12.7g

QUINOA HOT BREAKFAST CEREAL

Ingredients:

1 cup brown basmati rice	1/2 cup sesame seeds
1/2 cup quinoa	1/2 cup flax seeds
1/2 cup millet	1/2 cup cornmeal
1/2 cup buckwheat groats	1/2 cup amaranth

Directions:

1   Grind the basmati rice in a coffee grinder until it resembles a coarse powder. Empty the ground rice into a bowl.

2   Repeat the process with the quinoa, millet, buckwheat, sesame seeds, and flax seeds. Stir in the cornmeal and amaranth.

3   Store in an air tight container in the refrigerator until ready to cook.

4   When ready to cook bring 4 cups of water and a pinch of salt to boil in a saucepan. Take 1 cup of cereal mix and stir it in the boiling water then reduce the heat to medium-low.

5   Stirring frequently simmer for 20 minutes. *Enjoy!*

PER SERVING - Calories:257kcal; Fat:8g; Saturated fat:1.1g; Cholesterol:0mg; Carbohydrate:40.8g; Sugar:0.6g; Fiber:6.3g; Protein:7.9g

QUINOA MUFFINS

Serves 6 / Prep time: 15 min / Cook time: 20 min / Total Time: 35 min

Ingredients:

extra-virgin (organic) olive oil spray	1/4 cup sliced mushrooms
1 cup cooked quinoa	1/4 cup chopped onion
3 large eggs, beaten	1/2 tsp. dried thyme
1/4 cup crumbled feta cheese	salt and ground black pepper to taste

Directions:

1. Preheat oven to 400 degrees Fahrenheit. Prepare 6 muffin cups with cooking spray.

2. Beat quinoa, eggs, feta cheese, mushrooms, onion, thyme, salt, and pepper together in a large bowl.

3. Spoon into prepared muffin cups to about halfway full.

4. Bake in the preheated oven until edges brown and the tops are firm to the touch, 20 to 30 minutes. *Enjoy!*

PER SERVING - Calories:94kcal; Fat:4.5g; Saturated fat:1.7g; Cholesterol:99mg; Carbohydrate:7.8g; Sugar: 0.8g; Fiber:1.1g; Protein:5.6g

POWER OATMEAL

Serves 1 / Prep time: 10 min / Cook time: - min / Total Time: 25 min

Ingredients:

1/4 cup quick cooking oats	1/4 banana, mashed
1/4 cup milk	2-1/4 tbsp. flax seeds meal
2 tablespoons Greek yogurt	1-1/2 tbsp. peanut butter

Directions:

1   Whisk oats, milk, yogurt, banana, flax seed meal, and peanut butter together in a bowl. Refrigerate until set, at least 15 minutes. *Enjoy!*

PER SERVING - Calories:242kcal; Fat:11.4g; Saturated fat:3.3g; Cholesterol:11mg; Carbohydrate:27.4g; Sugar:8.5g; Fiber:4.7g; Protein:9.5g

BLUEBERRY AND BANANA STEEL CUT OATS

Serves 1 / Prep time: 5 min / Cook time: 10 min / Total Time: 15 min

Ingredients:

1 small banana	1/4 tsp. ground ground cinnamon, or more to taste
1 cup almond milk	1 pinch salt
1 tablespoon honey	1/2 cup rolled oats

Directions:

1. In a saucepan mash half the banana. Whisk almond milk, ground cinnamon, honey and salt together with the mashed banana till smooth. Bring the mixture to a boil and stir oats into it.

2. Reduce the heat to a medium-low and cook at simmer till the oats are tender and the moisture is absorbed to consistency of your liking, 5 – 7 minutes. Transfer oatmeal to a serving bowl.

3. Dice the remaining half of the banana. Top oatmeal with diced banana and more ground cinnamon, as desired. *Enjoy!*

PER SERVING - Calories:385kcal; Fat:5.7g; Saturated fat:0.6g; Cholesterol:0mg; Carbohydrate:76.8g; Sugar:37.5g; Fiber:8.1g; Protein:7.6g

PUMPKIN OATMEAL

Serves 2 / Prep time: 5 min / Cook time: 3 min / Total Time: 8 min

Ingredients:

1 cup quick-cooking rolled oats

3/4 cup milk (unsweetened), or as needed

1/2 cup canned pumpkin puree

1/4 tsp. pumpkin pie spice

1 tsp. ground cinnamon

Directions:

1   Mix together oats and milk in a microwave-safe bowl. Cook on high for 1 to 2 minutes, stirring once.

2   Add more milk or oats to achieve the desired consistency, and cook for another 30 seconds.

3   Stir in pumpkin puree, pumpkin pie spice, and ground cinnamon.

4   Heat through, and serve. *Enjoy!*

PER SERVING - Calories:229kcal; Fat:4.7g; Saturated fat:1.6g; Cholesterol:7mg; Carbohydrate:38.7g; Sugar:6.8g; Fiber:6.8g; Protein:9.4g

NO-COOK OVERNIGHT OATMEAL

Serves 1 / Prep time: 5 min / Cook time: - min / Total Time: 8 hours

Ingredients:

1/3 cup milk	2 tbsp. honey
1/4 cup rolled oats	1 tsp. ground cinnamon
1/4 cup Greek yogurt	1/4 cup fresh blueberries
2 tbsp. chia seeds	

Directions:

1   Combine milk, oats, Greek yogurt, chia seeds, honey, and cinnamon in a 1/2-pint jar with a lid.

2   Cover and shake until combined.

3   Remove lid and fold in blueberries. Cover jar with lid.

4   Refrigerate oatmeal, 8 hours to overnight. *Enjoy!*

PER SERVING - Calories:279kcal; Fat:9.6g; Saturated fat:3.9g; Cholesterol:18mg; Carbohydrate:41.1g; Sugar:21.9g; Fiber:6.1g; Protein:9.5g

HEARTY APPLE ALMOND OATMEAL

Serves 1 / Prep time: 10 min / Cook time: - min / Total Time: 10 min

Ingredients:

1 oz. rolled oats

1/2 cup hot milk or water

1 tablespoon natural almond butter

1 red apple, cored and roughly chopped

1/4 cup whole natural almonds

1/2 tsp. cinnamon

2 tbsp. honey

Directions:

1   Put rolled oats into a small serving bowl.

2   Add hot milk or water and almond butter. Stir until satisfied with consistency of the mix (approx.15 sec)

3   Top with chopped apples, almonds, cinnamon and honey. *Enjoy!*

PER SERVING - Calories:594kcal; Fat:31.9g; Saturated fat:4.3g; Cholesterol:10mg; Carbohydrate:67.6g; Sugar:35.3g; Fiber:11.6g; Protein:18g

PORTOBELLO PESTO EGG OMELETTE

Serves 1 / Prep time: 10 min / Cook time: 15 min / Total Time: 25 min

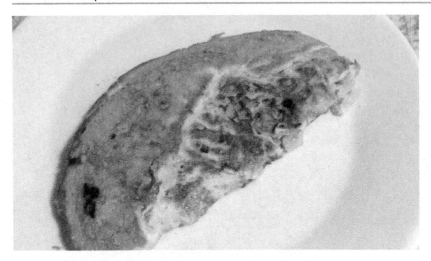

Ingredients:

1 tsp. extra-virgin olive oil

1 Portobello mushroom cap, sliced

1/4 cup chopped red onion

4 egg whites

1 tsp. water

salt and ground black pepper to taste

1/4 cup shredded low-fat mozzarella cheese

1 tsp. prepared pesto

Directions:

1   Over medium heat in a skillet heat the olive oil. In the heated olive oil cook together Portobello mushroom cap and red onion till the mushroom has been softened, 3 – 5 minutes.

2   Whisk the egg whites and water together in a small bowl; pour over the mushroom and onion mixture. Season the egg whites with salt and pepper.

3   Cook, stirring occasionally, until the egg whites are no longer runny, about 5 minutes.

4   Sprinkle the mozzarella cheese over the mixture; top with the pesto. Fold the omelette in half and continue cooking until the cheese melts, 2 to 3 minutes. *Enjoy!*

PER SERVING - Calories:259kcal; Fat:12g; Saturated fat:4.2g; Cholesterol:19mg; Carbohydrate:12g; Sugar:4.7g; Fiber:2.5g; Protein:28g

ZUCCHINI EGG WHITE FRITTATA

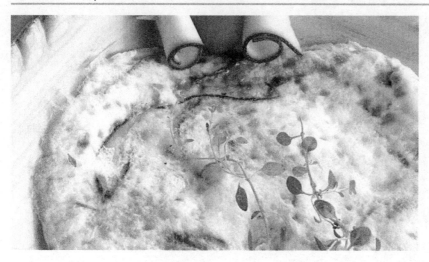

Ingredients:

1 tsp. extra-virgin olive oil	4 egg whites
1 tablespoon minced shallot	kosher salt to taste
1/2 clove garlic, minced	1/2 tsp. chopped fresh thyme
1 small zucchini, shaved into thin strips	ground black pepper to taste

Directions:

1   Heat olive oil in a non-stick skillet over medium heat. Cook and stir shallot and garlic in the hot oil until softened, about 5 minutes.

2   Add zucchini. Cook, stirring occasionally, until tender, about 5 minutes.

3   Whisk egg whites, salt, and thyme together in a small bowl. Mix into zucchini mixture.

4   Cook, undisturbed, over low heat until frittata is set, about 2 minutes. Flip frittata and cook for one more minute. Season with salt and pepper. *Enjoy!*

PER SERVING - Calories:137kcal; Fat:5g; Saturated fat:0.7g; Cholesterol:0mg; Carbohydrate:7.9g; Sugar:3.3g; Fiber:1.7g; Protein:16.5g

CRUSTLESS SPINACH QUICHE

Serves 6 / Prep time: 20 min / Cook time: 30 min / Total Time: 50 min

Ingredients:

1 tablespoon extra-virgin olive oil

1 onion, chopped

1 (10 oz.) package frozen chopped spinach, thawed and drained

5 eggs, beaten

3 cups shredded Muenster cheese

1/4 tsp. salt

1/8 tsp. ground black pepper

Directions:

1   Preheat the oven to 350 degrees Fahrenheit. Softly grease 9-inch pie pan.

2   In a large skillet heat the olive oil over medium-high heat. Add chopped onions and cook, stirring often, till onions are soft. Stir in spinach and go on cooking till the extra moisture has evaporated.

3   Use a large bowl to combine eggs, cheese, salt, pepper and spinach mixture. Stir to blend. Scoop into the prepared pie pan.

4   Bake in the preheated oven till the eggs have set, around 30 minutes. Let it cool down for 10 minutes before serving. *Enjoy!*

PER SERVING - Calories:309kcal; Fat:23.7g; Saturated fat:12.5g; Cholesterol:209mg; Carbohydrate:4.8g; Sugar:2.1g; Fiber:1.6g; Protein:20.4g

SPINACH SALAD WITH WARM BACON-MUSTARD DRESSING

Serves 4 / Prep time: 15 min / Cook time: 5 min / Total Time: 20 min

Ingredients:

1 (10 oz.) bag baby spinach leaves	1 tsp. garlic, minced
1 cup sliced mushrooms	1 large shallot, minced
10 ounces Swiss cheese, shredded	1/3 cup white wine vinegar
4 strips crisply cooked bacon, crumbled	1/3 cup honey
4 hard-cooked eggs, peeled and sliced	1/3 cup Dijon mustard
1/2 cup toasted sliced almonds	2 strips crisply cooked bacon, crumbled
1 tablespoon extra-virgin olive oil	salt and pepper to taste

Directions:

1   In a large serving bowl combine spinach, mushrooms, Swiss cheese, 4 crumbled strips of bacon, hard-cooked eggs and almonds.

2   Over medium heat in a small skillet heat olive oil. Stir in the garlic and shallots and cook till tender and translucent, around 2 minutes.

3   Whisk in the vinegar, honey, Dijon mustard, 2 crumbled strips of bacon and season to taste with salt and pepper. Cook until hot.

4   Over spinach mixture pour the hot dressing and toss to coat. *Enjoy!*

PER SERVING - Calories:663kcal; Fat:40.6g; Saturated fat:17.2g; Cholesterol:293mg; Carbohydrate:40.1g; Sugar:26g; Fiber:3.1g; Protein:36.1g

ASPARAGUS MUSHROOM BACON CRUSTLESS QUICHE

Serves 8 / Prep time: 15 min / Cook time: 40 min / Total Time: 55 min

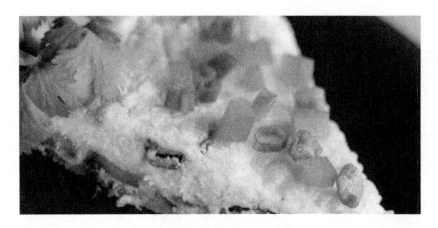

Ingredients:

6 ounces bacon, diced

1/2 lbs. asparagus, cut into 1-inch pieces

4 oz. baby bella (cremini) mushrooms, sliced

4 oz. shredded Swiss cheese

1 1/2 cups heavy whipping cream

4 large eggs

1/4 tsp. salt

freshly ground black pepper to taste

Directions:

1   Position oven rack to center position. Preheat oven to 400 degrees Fahrenheit. Butter a 10-inch pie plate.

2   Heat a large skillet over medium heat. Cook and stir bacon in the hot skillet until crisp, 5 to 10 minutes. Remove bacon and drain all but 2 tablespoons grease from skillet.

3   Cook and stir asparagus and mushrooms in the remaining bacon grease until asparagus is tender, about 5 minutes.

4   Remove skillet from heat and toss bacon into asparagus mixture. Spread asparagus-bacon mixture into the prepared pie pan. Sprinkle Swiss cheese over mixture.

5   Whisk cream, eggs, salt, and pepper in a bowl. Pour egg mixture over asparagus-cheese mixture.

6   Bake in the preheated oven until quiche is set and a knife inserted in the center comes out clean, about 30 minutes. *Enjoy!*

PER SERVING - Calories:291kcal; Fat:25.9g; Saturated fat:14.6g; Cholesterol:175mg; Carbohydrate:3.9g; Sugar:1.2g; Fiber:0.8g; Protein:11.5g

CUCUMBER-AVOCADO SANDWICH

Serves 1 / Prep time: 10 min / Cook time: - min / Total Time: 10 min

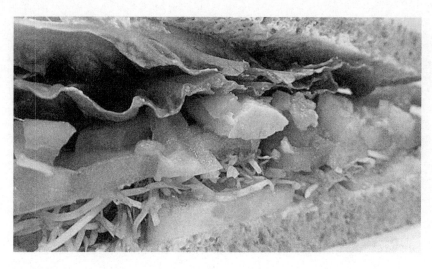

2 thick slices whole wheat bread

2 tablespoons cream cheese, softened

6 slices cucumber

2 tablespoons alfalfa sprouts

1 tsp. red wine vinegar

1 tsp. extra-virgin olive oil

1 tomato, sliced

1 leaf lettuce

1 ounce pepperoncini, sliced

1/2 avocado, mashed

Directions:

1   Cover each slice of bread with 1 tablespoon cream cheese. On one slice of bread, arrange cucumber slices in a single layer. Top with sprouts, then sprinkle with vinegar and oil.

2   Layer tomato slices, lettuce, and pepperoncini. Cover other slice of bread with mashed avocado.

3   Close sandwich and serve immediately. *Enjoy!*

PER SERVING - Calories:292kcal; Fat:32.5g; Saturated fat:9.8g; Cholesterol:32mg; Carbohydrate:46.3g; Sugar:4g; Fiber:12.3g; Protein:11.4g

DELICIOUS AVOCADO SANDWICH

Serves 1 / Prep time: 10 min / Cook time: - min / Total Time: 10 min

2 slices of Ezekiel or whole-wheat
bread of your choice

1/2 tomato, sliced

2 slices mozzarella cheese

1 1/2 tbsp. balsamic vinegar

1/4 avocado - peeled, pitted, and thinly
sliced

Directions:

1   Lay 1 slice bread on a plate. Place mozzarella cheese on bread and top with avocado and tomato slices, respectively.

2   Drizzle balsamic vinegar over tomato and top with remaining slice of bread. *Enjoy!*

PER SERVING - Calories:428kcal; Fat:24.2g; Saturated fat:11.1g; Cholesterol:39mg; Carbohydrate:34.4g; Sugar:5.5g; Fiber:5.3g; Protein:19.9g

AVOCADO AND ORANGE SANDWICH

Serves 4 / Prep time: 10 min / Cook time: - min / Total Time: 10 min

Ingredients:

8 (1 oz.) slices Ezekiel or whole-wheat
bread of your choice

1 large navel orange, peeled and
cut into 1/4-inch thick slices

2 large avocados - peeled, pitted, and
sliced

1 (5 oz.) package alfalfa sprouts

2 tbsp. balsamic vinaigrette

Directions:

1   Arrange four of the bread slices on a flat surface. Top each slice with two slices of orange, even amounts of avocado slices, and even amounts of sprouts.

2   Sprinkle each sandwich with 1/2 tsp. of balsamic vinaigrette.

3   Top each with remaining bread slices and serve. *Enjoy!*

PER SERVING - Calories:407kcal; Fat:23.7g; Saturated fat:3.5g; Cholesterol:0mg; Carbohydrate:42.6g; Sugar:8.6g; Fiber:15.3g; Protein:12g

AVOCADO PROSCIUTTO HAM SANDWICH

Serves 1 / Prep time: 15 min / Cook time: - min / Total Time: 15 min

Ingredients:

1/2 ripe avocado, pitted

2 slices pumpernickel bread, toasted

1/4 cup canned garbanzo beans, rinsed and drained

1 pinch salt

1 slice prosciutto

1 1/2 slices tomato

1 slice Havarti cheese

1/4 cup alfalfa sprouts

Directions:

1   On one slice of toasted pumpernickel bread spread the avocado. On top of the avocado place garbanzo beans and sprinkle with salt.

2   Layer with prosciutto, tomato, Havarti cheese, and alfalfa sprouts.

3   To make a sandwich cover that with another slice of bread. *Enjoy!*

PER SERVING Calories:582kcal; Fat:33.3g; Saturated fat:11.4g; Cholesterol:48mg; Carbohydrate:55.1g; Sugar:2.1g; Fiber:14.5g; Protein:20.8g

LEMON AVOCADO TOAST

Serves 2 / Prep time: 10 min / Cook time: 5 min / Total Time: 15 min

Ingredients:

2 slices of Ezekiel or whole-wheat bread of your choice

1/2 avocado

2 tablespoons chopped fresh cilantro, or more to taste

1 tsp. lemon juice, or to taste

1/4 tsp. lemon zest

1 pinch cayenne pepper

1 pinch fine sea salt

1/4 tsp. chia seeds

Directions:

1   Toast bread slices to your desired liking, 3 - 5 minutes.

2   Mash avocado in a bowl. Stir in cilantro, lemon juice, lemon zest, cayenne pepper, and sea salt.

3   Spread avocado mixture onto the toast and cover with chia seeds. *Enjoy!*

PER SERVING Calories:84kcal; Fat:2.3g; Saturated fat:0.4g; Cholesterol:0mg; Carbohydrate:12.4g; Sugar:1.8g; Fiber:2.7g; Protein:3.8g

HUMMUS AND PROSCIUTTO WRAP

Serves 4 / Prep time: 15 min / Cook time: 8 min / Total Time: 23 min

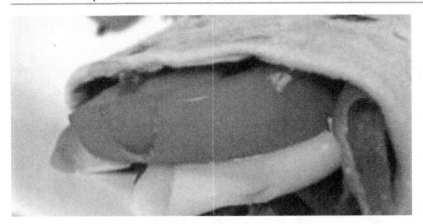

Ingredients:

12 thin slices prosciutto	1 avocado - peeled, pitted, and sliced – divided
4 10-inch low carb whole wheat tortillas	4 small tomatoes, sliced
1/2 cup hummus spread, divided	1 cup torn lettuce leaves, divided
4 slices mozzarella cheese	

Directions:

1   Preheat the oven to 350 degrees Fahrenheit. Using parchment paper to line a baking sheet.

2   In a way that they don't touch on the baking sheet spread out the prosciutto slices. Bake them in the preheated oven until crisp, 6 – 8 minutes. Move them from the oven and let them cool down.

3   Layer tortillas on a plate. Place them in the microwave and heat them on "High" till warmed and pliable, 20 – 30 seconds.

4   Spread 2 tablespoons of hummus on each tortilla. Layer each tortilla with 3 slices of crisped prosciutto. Top that with a slice of mozzarella cheese and on the cheese spread 1/4 of the avocado slices. Finish each tortilla wrap with 1 sliced tomato and about 1/4 cup of torn lettuce leaves.

5   To enclose the filling fold the bottom of each tortilla up about 2 inches, and roll them firmly into a compact cylinder. *Enjoy!*

PER SERVING Calories:345kcal; Fat:23.4g; Saturated fat:6.9g; Cholesterol:37mg; Carbohydrate:24g; Sugar:3.3g; Fiber:14.3g; Protein:20g

BLACK BEAN AND COUSCOUS SALAD

Serves 8 / Prep time: 35 min / Cook time: - min / Total Time: 35 min

Ingredients:

1 cup uncooked couscous	1 red bell pepper, seeded and chopped
1 1/4 cups chicken broth	1/4 cup chopped fresh cilantro
2 tablespoons fresh lime juice	8 green onions, chopped
3 tablespoons extra-virgin olive oil	1 cup frozen corn kernels, thawed
1/2 tsp. ground cumin	2 (15 oz.) cans black beans, drained
1 tsp. red wine vinegar	salt and pepper to taste

Directions:

1   In a 2 quart or larger saucepan bring chicken broth to a boil and stir in the couscous. Cover the saucepan and remove from heat. Let it cool down for 5 minutes.

2   In a large bowl, whisk together lime juice, olive oil, cumin and vinegar. Add red pepper, cilantro, green onions, corn and beans. Toss to coat.

3   Break up any chunks by fluffing the couscous well. Add fluffed couscous to the bowl with vegetables and mix well.

4   Season to taste with salt and pepper and serve at once or refrigerate till ready to serve. *Enjoy!*

PER SERVING Calories:255kcal; Fat:5.9g; Saturated fat:0.8g; Cholesterol:0mg; Carbohydrate:41.2g; Sugar:1.9g; Fiber:9.7g; Protein:10.4g

<u>ALMOND BERRY SMOOTHIE</u>

Serves 1 / Prep time: 10 min / Cook time: - min / Total Time: 10 min

Ingredients:

1 banana

1 cup frozen blueberries

1 tablespoon almond butter

1/2 cup natural almond milk, unsweetened

water as needed

Directions:

1   Place banana, blueberries, almond butter and almond milk in a blender.

2   Blend till smooth. Add in a little water for a thinner smoothie. *Enjoy!*

PER SERVING Calories:321kcal; Fat:11.7g; Saturated fat:1.1g; Cholesterol:0mg; Carbohydrate:55.6g; Sugar:33.4g; Fiber:7.7g; Protein:5.3g

RASPBERRY BLACKBERRY SMOOTHIE

Serves 2 / Prep time: 10 min / Cook time: - min / Total Time: 10 min

Ingredients:

1 (6 oz.) container vanilla yogurt	1/2 cup blackberries
1 tablespoon honey	1 small banana
1 cup fresh raspberries	4 ice cubes

Directions:

1   Place yogurt, honey, raspberries, blackberries, banana and ice cubes into a blender.

2   Blend till smooth. *Enjoy!*

PER SERVING Calories:195kcal; Fat:1.7g; Saturated fat:0.8g; Cholesterol:4mg; Carbohydrate:42.5g; Sugar:31.1g; Fiber:7.3g; Protein:5.8g

BANANA GREEN SMOOTHIE

Serves 1 / Prep time: 5 min / Cook time: - min / Total Time: 5 min

Ingredients:

2 cups baby spinach leaves, or to taste

1 banana

1 carrot, peeled and cut into large chunks

3/4 cup plain fat-free Greek yogurt, or to taste

3/4 cup ice

2 tablespoons honey

Directions:

1   Place spinach, banana, carrot, yogurt, ice, and honey in a blender.

2   Blend till smooth. *Enjoy!*

PER SERVING Calories:364kcal; Fat:0.8g; Saturated fat:0.2g; Cholesterol:0mg; Carbohydrate:77.4g; Sugar:59.4g; Fiber:6.5g; Protein:18.6g

VEGAN STRAWBERRY OATMEAL SMOOTHIE

Serves 2 / Prep time: 10 min / Cook time: - min / Total Time: 10 min

Ingredients:

1 cup natural almond milk

1/2 cup rolled oats

14 frozen strawberries

1 banana, broken into chunks

Directions:

1   Place almond milk, oats, strawberries, banana, agave nectar, and vanilla extract in a blender.

2   Blend till smooth. *Enjoy!*

PER SERVING Calories:205kcal; Fat:2.9g; Saturated fat:0.3g; Cholesterol:0mg; Carbohydrate:42.4g; Sugar:18.4g; Fiber:5.9g; Protein:4.2g

QUICK MEDITERRANEAN
LUNCH RECIPES

Just because you are on the go does not mean that you cannot enjoy a tasty exotic meal. Prepare any one of these recipes earlier during the day and heat them up at your office pantry for a sumptuous Mediterranean lunch. They are also easy to whip up during your lazy lunchtime days.

EFFORTLESS TUNA

Serves 4 / Prep time: 15 min / Cook time: 10 min / Total Time: 25 min

Ingredients:

2 eggs

2 tbsp. lemon juice

3 tbsp. grated Parmesan cheese

10 tbsp. Italian-seasoned bread crumbs

3 (5 oz.) tuna caned in water, drained

3 tbsp. diced onion

1 pinch ground black pepper

3 tbsp. extra-virgin olive oil

Directions:

1   Beat eggs and lemon juice in a bowl. Stir in Parmesan cheese and bread crumbs to make a paste.

2   Fold in tuna and onion until well-mixed. Season with black pepper. Shape tuna mixture into eight 1-inch-thick patties.

3   Heat olive oil in a skillet over medium heat; fry patties until golden brown, about 5 minutes per side. *Enjoy!*

PER SERVING Calories:325kcal; Fat:15.5g; Saturated fat:3.2g; Cholesterol:125mg; Carbohydrate:13.9g; Sugar:1.2g; Fiber:0.8g; Protein:31.3g

YUMMY TUNA BURGERS

Serves 4 / Prep time: 22 min / Cook time: 8 min / Total Time: 30 min

Ingredients:

1/2 cup Italian seasoned bread crumbs

1 egg

1 (5 oz.) tuna caned in water, drained

1/3 cup minced onion

1/4 cup minced red bell pepper

1/4 cup minced celery

1/4 cup mayonnaise

1/2 tsp. dried dill weed

2 tablespoons chili sauce

1/4 tsp. salt

1/8 tsp. ground black pepper

1 dash Worcestershire sauce

4 whole wheat hamburger buns

1 tomato, sliced

4 leaves of lettuce optional

Directions:

1   Mix together bread crumbs, egg, tuna, onion, red bell pepper, celery, mayonnaise, dill, chili sauce, salt, pepper, and Worcestershire sauce. Mix together well.

2   Shape into 4 patties (mixture will be very delicate and soft). To make patties easier to handle refrigerate them for 30 minutes, if desired.

3   With a cooking spray coat a non-stick skillet. Fry tuna patties for around 3 – 4 minutes per side, or until cook through. Be careful when turning them because they are fragile.

4   Serve on buns with lettuce leaves and tomato slices. *Enjoy!*

PER SERVING Calories:353kcal; Fat:15.6g; Saturated fat:2.8g; Cholesterol:61mg; Carbohydrate:36.6g; Sugar:3.3g; Fiber:3g; Protein:16.4g

SALAD NICOISE

Serves 4 / Prep time: 30 min / Cook time: 15 min / Total Time: 45 min

Ingredients:

1/2 pound new potatoes, quartered	1/2 pound mixed salad greens
1/4 cup pitted nicoise olives	1 cup lemon vinaigrette
1/4 cup chopped fresh parsley	3 roma (plum) tomatoes, thinly sliced
1 (5 oz.) tuna caned in water, drained	3 hard-cooked eggs, quartered
1/2 onion, thinly sliced	1 tablespoon capers
1/3 pound fresh green beans - rinsed, trimmed and blanched	4 anchovy filets

Directions:

1   Bring salted water to a boil in a large pot. Put in potatoes, and cook till tender but still firm, around 15 minutes. Drain and let it cool down.

2   Combine in a large bowl potatoes, olives, parsley, tuna, onion and green beans. Refrigerate for 2 – 4 hours.

3   Toss in large bowl greens with vinaigrette and cover with chilled potato mixture.

4   Decorate with tomatoes, eggs, capers and anchovies. *Enjoy!*

PER SERVING Calories:287kcal; Fat:8.7g; Saturated fat:1.9g; Cholesterol:172mg; Carbohydrate:34.7g; Sugar:17.2g; Fiber:4.4g; Protein:17.5g

PLEASURABLE TUNA

Serves 4 / Prep time: 10 min / Cook time: 20 min / Total Time: 30 min

Ingredients:

1 (20 oz.) package frozen roasted red potatoes

1 (12 oz.) package frozen whole green beans

4 large eggs

3/4 cup dry-packed sun-dried tomatoes, halved

3 tablespoons white balsamic or white wine vinegar

1 tablespoon Dijon mustard

1/4 tsp. salt

1/4 tsp. black pepper

1/4 tsp. dried thyme

1/3 cup extra-virgin olive oil

2 (5 oz.) tuna caned in water, drained

1/2 cup pitted Kalamata olives

Directions:

1   Cook potatoes and beans according to package directions.

2   Meanwhile, put eggs in a saucepan, cover with cold water, and bring to a boil. Cover, remove from heat, and let stand 12 minutes. Drain, run eggs under cold water, and peel. Halve each lengthwise.

3   Blanch tomatoes in a pot of boiling water to soften, 30 seconds. Drain well.

4   Whisk together vinegar, mustard, salt, pepper, and thyme in a bowl. Gradually add oil, whisking until combined well.

5   Arrange potatoes, beans, tomatoes, eggs, tuna, and olives on a platter and drizzle dressing over top. *Enjoy!*

PER SERVING Calories:599kcal; Fat:33g; Saturated fat:5.6g; Cholesterol:198mg; Carbohydrate:45.3g; Sugar:8g; Fiber:6.2g; Protein:31.7g

SPINACH AND SARDINE SANDWICH

Serves 1 / Prep time: 10 min / Cook time: - min / Total Time: 10 min

Ingredients:

2 tbsp. extra-virgin olive oil

1 small garlic clove, minced

2 ounces baby spinach 2 cups tightly packed, rinsed

Salt

freshly ground pepper

1 small (3 1/2-inch) whole-wheat English muffin, lightly toasted

Dijon mustard (optional)

2 canned sardines, preferably lightly smoked in olive oil about 2 ounces, filleted

1 small tomato, sliced optional

Lemon juice

About 1 tsp. mayonnaise

Directions:

1   Over medium heat in a medium skillet heat the olive oil, and then add the garlic. Cook by stirring till fragrant, around 30 seconds.

2   Turn up the heat and add the spinach. Wilt the spinach in the water left on the leaves after washing. Take off from the heat and season with salt and pepper. Press out and drain excess water.

3   Toast the English muffin, lightly. If desired, spread a little mustard over the bottom half and cover with the spinach. Place the sardine fillets on top of the spinach, and douse with a little lemon juice.

4   Over the sardines lay a nice ripe season tomato, if you desire. Spread the mayonnaise over the top half of the English muffin, and top the sandwich. Press down and slice in half or wrap and refrigerate until ready to eat. *Enjoy!*

PER SERVING Calories:409kcal; Fat:23g; Saturated fat:3g; Cholesterol:83mg; Carbohydrate:29g; Sugar:5g; Fiber:5g; Protein:21g

SARDINE AND POTATO SALAD WITH ARUGULA

Serves 4 / Prep time: 10 min / Cook time: 25 min / Total Time: 35 min

Ingredients:

1 1/2 pounds fingerling potatoes, halved lengthwise	1/4 tsp. smoked paprika
1 tsp. kosher salt, divided	1 large garlic clove, minced
5 tablespoons extra-virgin olive oil, divided	8 fresh whole sardines (about 1 pound)
Cooking spray	5 ounces baby arugula
3 tablespoons fresh lemon juice	8 lemon wedges
2 tablespoons minced shallots	Freshly ground black pepper

Directions:

1   Preheat the oven to 400 degrees Fahrenheit.

2   Mix potatoes, 3/8 teaspoon salt, and 1 tablespoon olive oil on a baking sheet coated with cooking spray. Toss well to coat.

3   Bake for 15 minutes. Stir potatoes and continue baking for additional 10 minutes or until golden brown and tender.

4   In a large bowl mix 2 tablespoons of olive oil, lemon juice, shallots, paprika, garlic, and 2/8 teaspoons of salt. Stir with a whisk. Add hot potatoes to the bowl and toss to coat.

5   In a large non-stick skillet heat the remaining 2 tablespoons of olive oil over medium-high heat. Pat sardines dry with paper towels and sprinkle with remaining 3/8 teaspoons

of salt. Place sardines to skillet and cook for 3 minutes on each side or till crispy and done.

6   Place about 1 1/2 cups of arugula on each of 4 plates. Add about 3/4 cup of potatoes mix on each serving. Top each serving with 2 sardines and serve with lemon wedge, sprinkle with pepper. *Enjoy!*

PER SERVING Calories:347kcal; Fat:19.1g; Saturated fat:2.7g; Cholesterol:23mg; Carbohydrate:33.3g; Sugar:5g; Fiber:2.6g; Protein:9.1g

PAN-FRIED SARDINES

Serves 5 / Prep time: 10 min / Cook time: 45min / Total Time: 55 min

Ingredients:

2 medium yellow onions	1/3 cup extra-virgin olive oil, divided
1 cup red-wine vinegar	About 1 tsp. kosher salt, divided
1/3 cup golden raisins	1/3 cup toasted pine nuts
2 pounds sardines, gutted, heads off*	3 tablespoons coarsely chopped flat-leaf parsley
1/3 cup whole-wheat flour	

Directions:

1   Slice onions into thin half-moons. Combine vinegar and raisins in a measuring cup. Rinse sardines well inside and out, dry with paper towels, and roll in flour, shaking off excess.

2   Heat 3 tbsp. oil in a large frying pan over medium heat. Fry sardines in 2 batches, 1 1/2 minutes per side, being careful not to overcook. Transfer to a large shallow serving dish or platter and sprinkle with 1/2 tsp. salt (you can layer the sardines if necessary).

3   Wipe pan clean with paper towels, return to heat, and add remaining oil. When oil is hot, add onions and remaining 1/2 tsp. salt. Cook, stirring often, until onions are a soft,

browned mass, 25 to 30 minutes.

4   Add vinegar and raisins and cook, stirring occasionally, 10 minutes. Pour over sardines and sprinkle with pine nuts. Let marinate for at least 1 hour at room temperature, covered, or chill for up to 4 days. Sprinkle with parsley to serve. *Enjoy!*

PER SERVING Calories:356kcal; Fat:24g; Saturated fat:3.7g; Cholesterol:49mg; Carbohydrate:16g; Sugar:11g; Fiber:1.5g; Protein:17g

HEARTY SALMON QUINOA BURGERS

Serves 5 / Prep time: 15 min / Cook time: 15 min / Total Time: 30 min

Ingredients for the burgers:

16 oz. wild salmon fillet, skin removed	freshly ground black pepper
1 tsp extra-virgin olive oil	3/4 cup cooked quinoa
1/3 cup diced shallots	2 tbsp. Dijon mustard
1 cup kale, chopped	1/2 tsp. Old Bay
Kosher salt, , to taste	1 large egg, beaten

Ingredients for the salad:

2 1/2 tbsp. extra-virgin olive oil	salt and pepper, to taste
2 1/2 tbsp. champagne vinegar	10 loose cups baby arugula
2 tbsp. minced shallots	1 large pink grapefruit, peeled and diced
1 1/4 tsp Dijon mustard	

Directions:

1. Whisk together in a small bowl the olive oil, shallots, Dijon, vinegar, salt and pepper.

2. Cut off from the salmon about 4 oz. piece and finely chop it in a food processor or chopper. This will help hold the burgers together.

3. Use the knife to finely chop the remaining salmon then transfer it to a large working bowl.

4. Add the olive oil in a large non-stick skillet and heat it over medium heat. Add shallots and kale in the heated skillet and saute them. Season with salt and pepper. Continue to cook over medium heat until tender and wilted, around 4 – 5 minutes.

5. Transfer it to the large working bowl with salmon along with quinoa, Dijon, Old Bay and egg. Mix well to combine. Form them into 5 patties, about 1/2 cup each.

6. Over medium heat add olive oil and lightly heat a non-stick grill pan or skillet. Start adding salmon patties. Cook from 4 – 5 minutes, then softly turn and cook an additional 4 – 5 minutes, or till cooked through.

7. Toss the dressing with grapefruit and arugula, divide among five plates.

8. Top each salad with a salmon burger. *Enjoy!*

PER SERVING Calories:277kcal; Fat:13g; Saturated fat:3.1g; Cholesterol:105mg; Carbohydrate:17g; Sugar:5g; Fiber:2g; Protein:23g

SALMON CROSTINI

Serves 6 / Prep time: 10 min / Cook time: 6 min / Total Time: 16 min

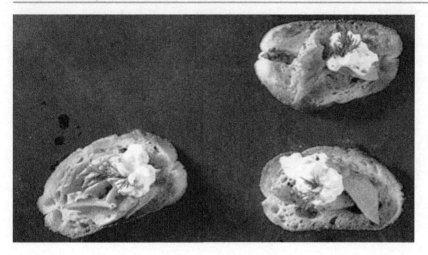

Ingredients:

1 (6-oz.) fresh or frozen sustainable sockeye salmon fillet (such as Alaskan)

1/4 tsp. freshly ground black pepper, divided

2 tablespoons finely chopped shallots

1 tablespoon chopped drained capers

3 tablespoons crème fraiche (alternative: sour cream)

1/4 tsp. grated lemon rind

1 tsp. fresh lemon juice

12 (1/2-oz.) slices diagonally cut whole-wheat French bread baguette, toasted

12 small dill sprigs

Directions:

1   Preheat broiler to high.

2   Place fillet on a foil-lined baking sheet; sprinkle fillet evenly with pepper. Broil 6 minutes or until desired degree of doneness. Cool 2 minutes; flake fillet.

3   Combine shallots and next 4 ingredients (through lemon juice) in a small bowl, stirring well. Place 2 toasted baguette slices on each of 6 small plates. Divide salmon evenly among baguette slices; top each crostini with 1 tsp. crème fraîche mixture and 1 dill sprig. *Enjoy!*

PER SERVING Calories:142kcal; Fat:4.3g; Saturated fat:2g; Cholesterol:49mg; Carbohydrate:16.7g; Sugar:1.5g; Fiber:0.8g; Protein:8.2g

POTATO BAKED SALMON

Serves 2 / Prep time: 30 min / Cook time: 20 min / Total Time: 50 min

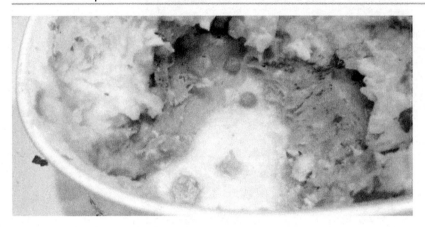

Ingredients for the salmon:

3/4 lbs. salmon fillet, fresh and without skin, about 1-1 1/2 inch thick

2 tablespoon parsley, chopped (preferably flat leaf)

salt, to taste

pepper, to taste

extra-virgin olive oil, for the casserole form

Ingredients for the mashed potatoes:

1/2 lbs. potato (like Yukon Gold)

2 tablespoons extra-virgin olive oil

2 medium onions, chopped

1/2 garlic clove, minced

1/2 cup low-fat milk (about)

1 pinch nutmeg

salt, to taste

Ingredients for the crust:

3 tablespoons breadcrumbs

1 tablespoon Parmesan cheese, grated

1 -3 tablespoon extra-virgin olive oil

Directions:

1   For fish: grease form. If necessary, cut fish into large pieces so that fish can be evenly put into casserole form. Salt and pepper to taste. Sprinkle 2 tbsp. parsley over salmon.

Set aside. Preheat oven to 375 degrees Fahrenheit.

2   For onions: cook chopped onions in olive oil until soft (for about 1-2 minutes).

3   Peel and cook potatoes in salted water for about 20 minutes until tender. Drain and mash potatoes. Add olive oil and add so much of the milk to have a spreadable consistency.

4   Add onions, garlic and nutmeg. Salt to taste.

5   Spread potatoes over fish.

6   Mix bread crumbs and parmesan. Add enough olive oil to moisten the crumbs. Sprinkle over the potatoes.

7   Bake in the middle of the oven for about 20 minutes until crust is golden brown. If it is getting to brown, cover it with aluminium foil.

8   Directly before serving sprinkle with chopped parsley. Serve immediately. *Enjoy!*

NOTE: Prepare fish and onions while potatoes are cooking.

PER SERVING Calories:650kcal; Fat:30.5g; Saturated fat:5.3g; Cholesterol:83.7mg; Carbohydrate:49.1g; Sugar:10g; Fiber:5.5g; Protein:44.5g

CHICKEN TOSTADOS

Serves 7 / Prep time: 10 min / Cook time: 45 min / Total Time: 55 min

Ingredients:

2 lbs. boneless skinless chicken thighs

1 cup barbecue sauce

4 1/2 oz. green chilies, chopped and drained

2 tomatoes, seeded and diced

1/2 small red onion, minced

1/4 cup chopped fresh cilantro

1 garlic clove, minced

1 tablespoon red wine vinegar

2 tbsp. extra-virgin olive oil

1/4 tsp. salt

8 (6 inch) whole-wheat tortillas

1 cup fat-free refried beans, canned

8 scallions, finely chopped

1 cup reduced-fat Monterey jack cheese, shredded

1/4 cup light sour cream

Directions:

1 Mix chicken, chilies and barbecue sauce in a large, non-stick saucepan. Bring the mix to a boil.

2 Lower the heat and simmer, covered, till the chicken is tender and cooked through, around 25 minutes. Remove from the heat and let it cool down.

3 In the meantime, mix well tomatoes, onion, chopped cilantro, garlic, vinegar, oil and salt in medium bowl until blended. Set aside.

4 Preheat the oven to 425 degrees Fahrenheit.

5 Use a cooking spray to spray a large, non-stick baking sheet.

6 Put tortillas on the baking sheet. Spread beans on each of them. Top the beans with chicken mixture, scallions, and cheese. Bake prepared tostada till the cheese is melted and bubbly, around 15 minutes.

7   Cover each tostada with tomato mixture, sour cream and extra cilantro, if desired. *Enjoy!*

PER SERVING Calories:307kcal; Fat:8.8g; Saturated fat:2.8g; Cholesterol:114.2mg; Carbohydrate:23.3g; Sugar:12.1g; Fiber:3g; Protein:32.6g

CHICKEN CORN SALAD

Serves 4 / Prep time: 10 min / Cook time: 25 min / Total Time: 35 min

Ingredients:

1 tablespoon Dijon mustard	1 jalapeño chili, seeded and minced
1/4 cup plus 1 tablespoon lemon juice	2 ears corn, kernels stripped
2 skinless and boneless chicken breasts, about 1 1/4 pounds, pounded thin	Salt and ground black pepper
3 tablespoons extra-virgin olive oil	1 medium yellow tomato, diced
1/2 cup chopped onion	1/3 cup flour
1 medium-size yellow summer squash, diced	2 tablespoons minced cilantro leaves

Directions:

1   In a shallow dish combine mustard and 1/4 cup lemon juice. Each chicken breast cut in half (lengthwise, so you get two thin filets) and put it in the mustard mixture. Coat both sides by turning filets and set aside.

2   In a large skillet heat 1 tablespoon olive oil. Add in onion and sauté on low for a few minutes, until softened. Add in squash, chili, and corn then continue to cook till the vegetables are tender, around 15 minutes. Season with salt and pepper. Remove from the heat. Add tomato and 1 tablespoon lemon juice. Set aside.

3   Remove the chicken from marinade, dust with flour. Season with salt and pepper. In a large cast-iron skillet or grill pan heat the remaining olive oil on medium-high heat. Sear

chicken, flipping once, till slightly browned and just cooked through, around 5 minutes per side. Place on the serving platter. Add cooking oil and cilantro to the salad. *Enjoy!*

PER SERVING Calories:449kcal; Fat:24g; Saturated fat:5g; Cholesterol:90mg; Carbohydrate:25g; Sugar:5g; Fiber:3g; Protein:34g

CHICKEN FRIED RICE

Serves 6 / Prep time: 10 min / Cook time: 15 min / Total Time: 25 min

Ingredients:

1 cooking spray	1/2 cup carrot, diced
4 large egg white	2 cup cooked brown rice, kept hot
1/2 cup scallion, chopped, green and white parts	1/2 cup frozen green peas, thawed
2 medium garlic cloves, minced	3 tbsp. low-sodium soy sauce
12 oz. boneless skinless boneless, skinless chicken breast, cut into 1/2-inch cubes	

Directions:

1   Use cooking spray to coat a large non-stick skillet and place it over medium-high heat. By stirring frequently, add in egg whites and cook, till scrambled, around 3 – 5 minutes. Remove from the skillet and set aside.

2   Again, use cooking spray to coat a large non-stick skillet and place it over medium-high heat. Add scallions and garlic then sauté for around 2 minutes. Add in chicken and carrots. Sauté till chicken is slightly golden brown and cooked through, around 5 minutes.

3   Stir in cooked egg whites you earlier set aside, cooked brown rice, peas and soy sauce.

4   Continue to cook till heated through, stirring once or twice, around 1 minute. *Enjoy!*

PER SERVING Calories:179kcal; Fat:2g; Saturated fat:0g; Cholesterol:36mg; Carbohydrate:21g; Sugar:2g; Fiber:3g; Protein:18g

CHICKEN AND PEPPER FAJITAS

Serves 4 / Prep time: 5 min / Cook time: 15 min / Total Time: 20 min

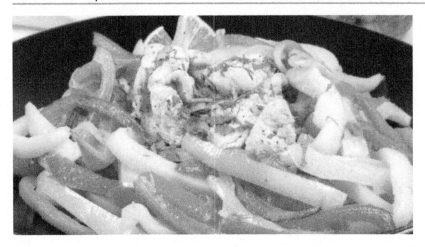

Ingredients:

2 tbsp. extra-virgin olive oil	2 bell pepper, sliced
8 oz. chicken cutlet, cut into 2-inch strips	1 medium onion, sliced
1 tsp. ground cumin	6 in flour tortilla, warmed
1/2 tsp. kosher salt	salsa, 1 sour cream, lime wedges, and sliced avocado for serving
2 clove garlic, chopped	1/4 tsp. black pepper

Directions:

1   In a large skillet heat 1 tablespoon of olive oil over medium-high heat. Use cumin, 1/2 teaspoon salt, 1/4 teaspoon black pepper, and cumin to season the chicken.

2   Add the seasoned chicken and garlic to the skillet and cook, turning occasionally, till cooked through, around 4 – 6 minutes. Transfer to the plate.

3   Use the remaining 1 tablespoon of olive oil and heat it in the skillet. Add bell peppers and onion and cook, tossing occasionally, till tender, around 6 – 8 minutes.

4   Add in the chicken and toss to combine. Serve in the tortillas with the salsa, sour cream, lime wedges, and avocado. *Enjoy!*

PER SERVING Calories:348kcal; Fat:13g; Saturated fat:3g; Cholesterol:31mg; Carbohydrate:39g; Sugar:4g; Fiber:4g; Protein:18g

CHICKEN SALAD WITH GRAPES

Serves 5 / Prep time: 10 min / Cook time: 21 min / Total Time: 31 min

Ingredients:

1 lbs. boneless, skinless chicken breasts, cooked, diced

1 cup celery, finely chopped

1 cup seedless grapes, halved

1 cup walnuts, or pecans (optional)

1 small onion, minced

1/2 tablespoon salt

1 tablespoon Worcestershire sauce

1/2 cup Miracle Whip topping

Directions:

1   Cook the perfect chicken breasts (See page 138)

2   Combine all ingredients in a bowl.

3   Serve with just about anything whole-wheat: crackers, tortilla chips, rolls, bread or bagel. *Enjoy!*

PER SERVING Calories:360kcal; Fat:25g; Saturated fat:4g; Cholesterol:59mg; Carbohydrate:15g; Sugar:9g; Fiber:2g; Protein:22g

SOUTHWESTERN CHICKEN SALAD

Serves 4 / Prep time: 20 min / Cook time: 21 min / Total Time: 41 min

Ingredients:

2 medium scallion, chopped

1/2 medium sweet red pepper, chopped

1/2 medium bell pepper, chopped

1 can (15 oz.) black beans, rinsed and drained

2 ear corn, kernels removed

2 tbsp. fresh lime juice

1 tbsp. extra-virgin olive oil

8 oz. chicken breast, cooked and chopped

2 tbsp. reduced-sodium taco seasoning mix

4 tbsp. fresh cilantro, chopped

4 tbsp. non-fat sour cream

Directions:

1   Cook the perfect chicken breasts (See page 139)

2   Combine scallions, peppers, beans and corn in large bowl; toss until well mixed.

3   Add lime juice and oil to bean mixture; toss to coat.

4   Add chicken, taco seasoning and cilantro; toss.

5   Top with sour cream and serve. *Enjoy!*

PER SERVING Calories:267kcal; Fat:4g; Saturated fat:1g; Cholesterol:40mg; Carbohydrate:38g; Sugar:5g; Fiber:9g; Protein:23g

TORTILLA COATED CHICKEN TENDERS

Serves 4 / Prep time: 5 min / Cook time: 20 min / Total Time: 25 min

Ingredients:

1 1/4 pound (8) boneless, skinless chicken breast tenders	1 tsp. garlic powder
1 tsp. kosher salt	1 tsp. cumin
Freshly ground black pepper, to taste	extra-virgin (organic) olive oil spray
1 large egg, lightly beaten	1/2 lime, cut into 4 wedges
2 tablespoons all-purpose flour (or gluten-free AP flour)	chopped fresh cilantro, for garnish
3 1/2 oz. crushed tortilla chips	1/2 cup jarred salsa, for dipping

Directions:

1 Preheat the oven to 400 degrees Fahrenheit.

2 Season chicken breast tenders with 3/4 teaspoon salt and pepper. Place egg in a medium bowl and flour on a shallow plate. Place tortilla chips, garlic powder, cumin, pepper, and the remaining 1/4 teaspoon of salt on another shallow plate.

3 Dredge each chicken breast tender lightly in flour, after that in egg (shaking of excess), next chip the mixture.

4 Use olive oil to lightly spray the sheet pan. Place the chicken breast tenders on pan and spray the top with olive oil. Bake around 8 – 10 minutes per side or till cooked through.

5 Arrange 2 chicken breast tenders on each plate and sprinkle with cilantro. Serve alongside with 1 lime wedge and salsa for dipping. *Enjoy!*

PER SERVING Calories:331kcal; Fat:11g; Saturated fat:2g; Cholesterol:137mg; Carbohydrate:22g; Sugar:2g; Fiber:1.5g; Protein:34g

CHICKEN WITH SESAME CUCUMBER RELISH

Serves 4 / Prep time: 10 min / Cook time: 20 min / Total Time: 30 min

Ingredients for cucumber relish:

1 tsp. toasted sesame oil

1 garlic clove, grated or finely minced

1/2 tsp. grated ginger

2 tbsp. (unseasoned) rice vinegar

1/4 tsp. kosher salt

3 tbsp. minced red onion

1 large English cucumber, seeded and diced

1 tbsp. toasted sesame seeds

Ingredients for the chicken:

1 lbs. (2) boneless, skinless chicken breast, cut lengthwise, into thin cutlets

2 tbsp. all-purpose gluten-free flour

1 large egg, lightly beaten

1 cup whole wheat panko breadcrumbs

1 tablespoon toasted sesame seeds

1/2 tsp. kosher salt, divided

freshly ground black pepper, to taste

extra-virgin (organic) olive oil spray

4 tsps. reduced sodium soy sauce

Directions:

1   Preheat the oven to 400 degrees Fahrenheit.

2   Using a small bowl, whisk together sesame oil, garlic, ginger, vinegar and salt. Add onion, cucumber, sesame seeds and stir. Set to the side and allow flavors to combine.

3   Use 1/4 teaspoon salt and pepper to season the chicken cutlets. Place an egg in a medium bowl and flour on a shallow plate. Place panko, sesame seeds, 1/4 teaspoon salt, pepper on another shallow plate.

4   Dredge each chicken cutlet lightly in the flour, next in the egg (shaking of excess) and finally in the panko mixture. Place on the sheet pan covered with parchment paper. Spray chicken cutlets lightly with olive oil and bake for around 20 minutes, rotating pan midway through.

5   Top each chicken cutlet with about 1/2 cup relish and 1 teaspoon soy sauce. *Enjoy!*

PER SERVING Calories:278kcal; Fat:8g; Saturated fat:2.3g; Cholesterol:119mg; Carbohydrate:21g; Sugar:4g; Fiber:1.5g; Protein:29g

STUFFED DELICATA SQUASH WITH CHICKEN

Serves 6 / Prep time: 15 min / Cook time: 30 min / Total Time: 45 min

Ingredients:

3 small delicata squash (about 16 ounces each), halved and seeded

extra-virgin (organic) olive oil spray

1/4 tsp. kosher salt

14 oz. sweet Italian chicken sausage

3/4 cup chopped onion

3/4 cup chopped celery

4 oz. chopped fresh shiitake mushrooms

1 sprig fresh thyme

6 tbsp. shredded parmesan cheese

chopped parsley, for garnish

Directions:

1   Preheat oven to 425 degrees Fahrenheit.

2   Spray the cut sides of the squash with oil and sprinkle with salt. Place face down on a large baking sheet. Bake until tender and browned on the edges, about 20 to 25 minutes.

3   Meanwhile, in a large sauté pan cook sausage on medium heat, breaking up the meat into small pieces as it cooks until the sausage is cooked through and is browned. Add the onion and celery. Cook until celery is soft, about 8 to 10 minutes.

4   Add the mushrooms and thyme to the pan, more salt and pepper if needed and cook, stirring 5 minutes, then cook covered for 2 minutes, or until the mushrooms are soft and cooked through.

5   Divide (1/2 cup) between the squash, top with parmesan cheese and bake 10 minutes. *Enjoy!*

PER SERVING Calories:240kcal; Fat:8g; Saturated fat:3.5g; Cholesterol:57mg; Carbohydrate:30.5g; Sugar:2.5g; Fiber:8g; Protein:15g

CORN AND CHICKEN SALAD WITH SALSA DRESSING

Serves 4 / Prep time: 5 min / Cook time: 10 min / Total Time: 15 min

Ingredients for the dressing:

1/2 cup jarred mild salsa

1/2 lime

4 tsps. extra-virgin olive oil

Ingredients for the chicken:

4 boneless, skinless chicken thighs (4 oz. each), trimmed of fat

3/4 tsp. kosher salt

1/4 tsp. dried oregano

1/4 tsp. cumin

Ingredients for the grilled salad:

2 corn on the cobs, husks removed

2 romaine hearts

extra-virgin (organic) olive oil spray

1/2 cup halved grape tomatoes

4 oz. avocado (1 small hass) sliced

2 tbsp. diced red onion

pinch of kosher salt

Directions:

6   Mix the salsa, lime juice, and olive oil. Set aside.

7   Season the chicken thighs.

8   Light up the grill to medium heat. From the romaine hearts remove any tired outer leaves and then halve each head vertically. Put on a large platter and with olive oil spray the cut sides. Also, lightly spray corn with olive oil.

9   Put chicken and corn on the grill and cook, till cooked through, around 5 minutes per side, till the corn is tender and the chicken is cooked through. When finished, transfer on a cutting board.

10   Grill romaine, cut side down, close to the heat source over high, around 1 – 2 minutes. Remove.

11   Cut the chicken into strips, remove the kernels off the corn and serve over Romaine with tomatoes, avocado, onions, salt and dressing on top. *Enjoy!*

PER SERVING Calories:288kcal; Fat:15.5g; Saturated fat:2.5g; Cholesterol:108mg; Carbohydrate:17g; Sugar:4g; Fiber:5g; Protein:25g

STUFFED TURKEY BREASTS WITH BUTTERNUT SQUASH

Serves 4 / Prep time: 15 min / Cook time: 47 min / Total Time: 62 min

Ingredients:

2 boneless turkey tenderloins (1 lbs. total)	5 black mission figs, chopped
1 tsp. kosher salt (diamond crystal)	1 cup baby spinach
1 tbsp. extra-virgin olive oil	3 sage leaves, chopped
1 small (1/3 cup) white onion, chopped	1/4 tsp. crushed black pepper
(6 oz.) 1 1/4 cups diced butternut squash, 1/2-inch dice	cooking twine – 6 to 8 pieces
2 garlic cloves, finely chopped	extra-virgin (organic) olive oil spray

Directions:

1   Preheat the oven to 375 degrees Fahrenheit.

2   Add olive oil in a large skillet and heat it over medium-high heat. Add onions and sauté for 2 minutes, or till golden. Add 2 tablespoons of water and butternut squash then cover with a lid. Cook on low heat for 10 minutes. Remove the cover and add garlic, figs, spinach, sage, salt, and pepper then cook for another 3 – 4 minutes. Set aside to cool down.

3   Into the sides of the tenderloins cut a pocket, be careful not to cut all the way through to the ends. Season with salt the inside and outside of the turkey.

4   With about 3/4 cup of squash mix stuff each turkey breast. Tie each breast with 3 – 4 pieces of twine (you will need to cut cooking twine long enough). Cut off extra twine.

5   Lightly spray skillet with cooking spray over medium-high heat. On each side carefully sear each turkey breast (Do not sear on stuff end). Cover with foil and put in the center of the oven, if your skillet is oven proof (If it is not oven proof, then move the breasts to the baking dish and cover with foil). Put directly into the oven and cook for 30 – 35 minutes.

6   Before cutting off twine and slicing turkey breasts in 4 slices, each, allow them to sit for 5 minutes. *Enjoy!*

PER SERVING Calories:258kcal; Fat:8g; Saturated fat:2.3g; Cholesterol:51mg; Carbohydrate:25g; Sugar:12g; Fiber:5g; Protein:22g

TURKEY LETTUCE WRAPS

Serves 4 / Prep time: 20 min / Cook time: 6 min / Total Time: 26 min

Ingredients for the turkey lettuce wraps:

1 tsp. extra-virgin olive oil

1/4 cup minced red bell peppers

1/4 cup minced scallions

12 oz. leftover turkey breast,
diced small (see page 138)

1/2 cup canned black beans, rinsed
and drained

2/3 cup frozen corn

2 tbsp. diced jarred jalapeno peppers

1/2 cup frozen spinach, thawed and
drained

1 tsp. cumin

1 tsp. chili powder

1/2 tsp. kosher salt

1 cup reduced fat shredded Mexican
cheese blend

8 large Iceberg lettuce leaves

12 tbsp. Avocado Cilantro Dressing

Ingredients for the Avocado Cilantro Dressing:

3/4 cup low-fat buttermilk

1 small jalapeno, seeds removed,
leave them in if you want it spicy

1/4 cup of fresh cilantro

1 medium hass avocado

1 clove garlic

2 tbsp. chopped scallion

juice of 1 lime

1/8 tsp. cumin

1/4 tsp. fresh ground pepper

1/2 tsp. kosher salt

Directions for the Avocado Cilantro Dressing:

1   In a blender mix all the ingredients, and blend till smooth.

2   Add more buttermilk for a thinner dressing, use less for a thicker one.

Directions for the turkey lettuce wraps:

3   Over medium-high heat in a large skillet heat the olive oil.

4   Add to the pan red bell pepper and scallions and sauté for about 2 minutes, until tender.

5   Add to the pan diced turkey, black beans, corn, jalapeno peppers, spinach, cumin, chili powder, salt and pepper. Continue cooking for another 3 – 4 minutes, stirring well so the spinach gets combined well with everything.

6   Put around 1/3 cup of turkey mix in the center of each lettuce leaf.

7   Cover each wrap with 2 tablespoon cheese and 1 1/2 tablespoon avocado sauce, if desired. *Enjoy!*

PER SERVING Calories:297kcal; Fat:13g; Saturated fat:3.5g; Cholesterol:53mg; Carbohydrate:21g; Sugar:4g; Fiber:6g; Protein:31g

LEFTOVER TURKEY TACOS

Serves 4 / Prep time: 14 min / Cook time: 1 min / Total Time: 15 min

Ingredients for the chicken:

1/2 tablespoon extra-virgin olive oil

2 tsps. lemon juice

Kosher salt

Freshly ground black pepper, to taste

8 medium Brussels sprouts, thinly sliced

(about 2 cups if using pre-shredded)

1/4 cup red onion, thinly sliced

8 whole-wheat tortillas

12 ounces leftover cooked skinless turkey, shredded and warmed (see page 138)

8 tbsp. cranberry pear sauce

Directions:

1   In a medium bowl, whisk together olive oil, lemon juice, 1/4 tsp. salt and pepper. Add Brussels sprouts and onion then toss to evenly coat.

2   Heat tortillas according to package directions. Top each tortilla with 1 1/2 oz. of turkey and 1/4 cup slaw. Top with cranberry sauce. *Enjoy!*

PER SERVING Calories:235kcal; Fat:5g; Saturated fat:1.7g; Cholesterol:37.5mg; Carbohydrate:30g; Sugar:9g; Fiber:4.6g; Protein:21.5g

TURKEY TORTILLAS

Serves 8 / Prep time: 20 min / Cook time: 30 min / Total Time: 50 min

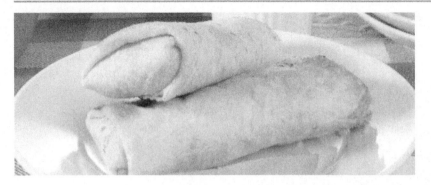

Ingredients:

1/2 lbs. ground turkey breast, uncooked

16 oz. canned fat-free refried beans

4 1/2 oz. canned mild green chili pepper,

drained and diced

1 3/4 cup salsa

1 tsp. chili powder

3 tbsp. scallion, thinly sliced

1 cup reduced-fat Monterey jack cheese, shredded

8 large burrito-size, whole-wheat tortilla

1 cup salsa

1/2 cup fat-free sour cream

1 extra-virgin (organic) olive oil spray

Directions:

1   Preheat the oven to 350 degrees Fahrenheit. With a cooking spray coat a large skillet and also coat 13 x 9 x 2 inch baking dish.

2   Over medium-high heat add turkey to skillet and cook till lightly browned, around 5 minutes. From the pan drain any excess liquid and then add beans, chili peppers, 1 3/4 salsa, chili powder, and scallions. Cook for around 3 minutes or till heated through. Stir in the cheese.

3   In the meantime, wrap tortillas in foil, and for 10 minutes warm them in the oven.

4   Spoon around 1/2 cup of turkey mixture onto each tortilla to assemble chimichangas, fold in sides and roll up.

5   In the, earlier, prepared baking dish place chimichangas. Bake tortillas uncovered till they are crisp and browned, around 20 minutes.

6   Top each with 2 tablespoons of salsa and 1 tablespoon of sour cream and serve. *Enjoy!*

PER SERVING Calories:366kcal; Fat:7g; Saturated fat:2g; Cholesterol:22mg; Carbohydrate:54g; Sugar:7g; Fiber:7g; Protein:22g

TACOS WITH TURKEY

Serves 6 / Prep time: 20 min / Cook time: 40 min / Total Time: 60 min

Ingredients:

1 (28-oz.) can chopped tomatoes with juice

1 tbsp. extra-virgin olive oil

1 medium onion, finely chopped

2 large garlic cloves, minced

1 lbs. ground turkey breast

1/4 tsp. ground black pepper

1 tsp. medium-hot chili powder (more to taste)

1 tsp. ground cinnamon

1/4 tsp. ground cloves

1/4 cup raisins

1 tbsp. plus 2 tsps. apple cider vinegar

Salt to taste

1 tart apple, peeled, cored and finely chopped

12 whole-wheat tortillas

2 cups shredded cabbage (about 6 oz.)

Salsa and crumbled as desired

Directions:

1   Use food processor fitted with the steel blade to pulse the canned tomatoes with juice till puréed. Set aside.

2   Over medium heat in a large heavy skillet heat the olive oil and add the onion. Cook the onion, stirring often, till it is tender, around 5 minutes. Add in the garlic and continue cooking, stirring often, till it is fragrant, around 30 seconds to a minute.

3   Increase the heat to medium-high and add the ground turkey. With salt and pepper season to taste and cook, stirring and breaking apart the meat, till it is lightly browned, around 8 minutes. Carefully pour off any liquid that the meat may have released into the pan. After you have done that, stir in the pepper, chili powder, cinnamon, cloves and raisins then stir together for around 1 minute.

4   Add in puréed tomatoes you set aside earlier, 1 tablespoon of vinegar and salt to taste then bring to a simmer. Simmer 15 minutes, stirring often, over medium-low heat. Add in the apple and continue to simmer for 10 more minutes, or till the mixture is thick and meaty. Taste and adjust the seasoning, if desired.

5   Use cold water to cover the cabbage and let it sit for 5 minutes. Drain and spin dry. Toss with the remaining vinegar. Heat the tortillas and spoon the picadillo onto each one. Cover with shredded cabbage, garnish with crumbled queso fresco and salsa, if desired. Serve. *Enjoy!*

PER SERVING Calories:390kcal; Fat:9g; Saturated fat:1g; Cholesterol:49mg; Carbohydrate:39g; Sugar:11g; Fiber:8g; Protein:21g

PORK AND ASPARAGUS

Serves 4 / Prep time: 5 min / Cook time: 30 min / Total Time: 35 min

Ingredients:

1/3 cup plus 2 tablespoons extra-virgin olive oil

1 1/4 lbs. pork tenderloin

1/2 tsp kosher salt, divided

3 shallot, cut into wedges

1 lbs. asparagus, tough ends trimmed

2 tbsp. apple cider vinegar

1 tbsp. whole-grain mustard

1/2 tsp black pepper, divided

Directions:

1   Preheat the oven to the 400 degrees Fahrenheit.

2   Over medium-high heat in a large ovenproof skillet heat 1 tablespoon of the olive oil.

3   With 1/4 teaspoon, each, salt and pepper season the pork. Add to skillet and cook, turning, till browned, around 5 – 6 minutes.

4   Move the skillet to the preheated oven and roast till the pork is cooked through, 12 – 15 minutes. Before slicing let it cool down for at least 5 minutes.

5   In the meantime, on a rimmed baking sheet, toss the shallots and asparagus with 1 tablespoon of olive oil and 1/4 teaspoon, each, salt and pepper.

6   Place the vegetables in a single layer and roast, tossing once, till tender, 12 – 15 minutes.

7   Whisk together in a bowl the vinegar, mustard, and the remaining 1/3 cup of olive oil.

8   Arrange the pork with the vegetables and drizzle with the vinaigrette and serve. *Enjoy!*

PER SERVING Calories:476kcal; Fat:32g; Saturated fat:6g; Cholesterol:111mg; Carbohydrate:8g; Sugar:4g; Fiber:2g; Protein:39g

BONELESS PORK CHOPS

Serves 4 / Prep time: 10 min / Cook time: 25 min / Total Time: 35 min

Ingredients:

16 oz. (8) thin sliced center cut boneless pork chops

3/4 tsp of McCormick Montreal Chicken Seasoning (25% less Sodium)

1 small (6 oz.) zucchini, ends trimmed off

1 small (6 oz.) yellow squash, ends trimmed off

1 cup halved grape tomatoes

1 tablespoon extra-virgin olive oil

1/4 tsp. kosher salt and fresh cracked pepper

1/4 tsp. oregano

3 garlic cloves, sliced thin

extra-virgin (organic) olive oil spray

1/4 cup of pitted and sliced Kalamata olives

1/4 cup of crumbled Feta cheese

fresh juice from 1/2 large lemon

1 tsp. grated lemon rind

Directions:

9   Preheat the oven to 450 degrees Fahrenheit. Use Montreal seasoning to season the pork chops, if desired (you can use any seasoned salt you like).

10   Slice the zucchini into 1/8-inch thick slices. Cut the slices into 1/8-inch thick strips, lengthwise.

11   Toss the tomatoes with 1/8 teaspoon salt and pepper, 1/2 tablespoon of the olive oil, and oregano.

12   Use cooking spray to lightly spray a baking dish and place tomatoes onto the dish, cut side down, roast for 10 minutes. Add sliced garlic and roast for another 5 minutes. When

80

finished, remove it to a large working bowl and set aside. Reduce the oven heat to 200 degrees Fahrenheit.

13   Heat over medium-high heat the remaining 1/2 tablespoon of olive oil in a large non-stick skillet. Add zucchini with 1/8 teaspoon salt and sauté till tender, around 5 minutes. Add it to the bowl with tomatoes and place all in the warm oven.

14   Working in two batches, cover the skillet bottom with cooking spray and cook on medium-high heat first half of the pork chops, around 1 1/2 – 2 minutes per side. Because the pork chops are thin you don't want to overcook them or they will be tough. Set aside on a platter.

15   Transfer the vegetables from the oven and mix with Kalamata olives, juice of lemon, and lemon rind. Top vegetables and pork chops with Feta cheese and serve. *Enjoy!*

PER SERVING Calories:230kcal; Fat:9g; Saturated fat:7g; Cholesterol:72mg; Carbohydrate:9g; Sugar:2g; Fiber:2g; Protein:28g

PORK SKEWERS

Serves 12 / Prep time: 14 min / Cook time: 6 min / Total Time: 20 min

Ingredients:

1 1/2 lbs. pork tenderloin, in half-inch slices

salt

pepper

2 tbsp. coriander seeds, lightly toasted and ground

2 tbsp. cumin seeds, lightly toasted and ground

1/2 tsp. dried oregano

1/2 tsp. pimentón, sweet or hot

2 garlic cloves

2 tbsp. extra-virgin olive oil

lemon wedges

Directions:

1   Put the pork slices onto 12 bamboo skewers. On both sides season lightly with salt and pepper.

2   Sprinkle the skewers with coriander, cumin, oregano, and pimentón. Smash the garlic cloves to a paste, add olive oil, and salt to taste. Mix it well and drizzle it over the meat. Using your fingers rub the seasoning into to the meat (the skewers can be refrigerated for several hours till ready to cook).

3   Over medium-high heat place a large cast-iron skillet or griddle. Cook the skewers for around 3 minutes per side, or till nicely browned.

4   Arrange with lemon wedges and a vegetable salad of your choice and serve. *Enjoy!*

PER SERVING Calories:91kcal; Fat:4g; Saturated fat:0g; Cholesterol:36mg; Carbohydrate:0g; Sugar:0g; Fiber:0g; Protein:11g

PORK TENDERLOIN APRICOT SALAD

Serves 4 / Prep time: 20 min / Cook time: 20 min / Total Time: 40 min

Ingredients:

1 pound pork tenderloin, trimmed	2 tablespoons minced shallot
1/2 tsp. salt, divided	2 tablespoons white-wine vinegar
1/4 tsp. freshly ground pepper, plus more to taste	2 tablespoons extra-virgin olive oil
3 tablespoons apricot preserves, divided	1 (4- to 5-oz.) bag watercress, or baby arugula (about 8 cups)
4 ripe but firm fresh apricots or nectarines, halved and pitted	

Directions:

1   Preheat the grill to high.

2   With 1/4 teaspoon of salt and pepper sprinkle the pork. Oil the grill rack. Turning occasionally, grill the pork, for around 10 minutes. Drizzle the pork with 2 tablespoon of apricot preserves and continue to grill till an instant-read thermometer inserted into the thickest part indicates 145 degrees Fahrenheit, 2 – 5 more minutes.

3   Grill, turning occasionally, apricot (or nectarine) halves on the coolest part of the grill, till marked and tender, around 4 minutes.

4   Move grilled pork and apricots (or nectarines) to a clean cutting board and let it cool down for 5 minutes.

5   In the meantime, in a large bowl, whisk the remaining 1 tablespoon preserves, shallot, vinegar, olive oil, 1/4 teaspoon salt and pepper to taste. Slice the fruit into wedges and add to the dressing together with watercress (or arugula). Toss to coat.

6   Thinly slice the pork and serve with salad. *Enjoy!*

PER SERVING Calories:247kcal; Fat:10g; Saturated fat:1g; Cholesterol:74mg; Carbohydrate:25g; Sugar:12g; Fiber:1g; Protein:25g

PORK TENDERLOIN WITH BLUE CHEESE

Serves 4 / Prep time: 15 min / Cook time: 15 min / Total Time: 30 min

Ingredients:

2 tablespoons extra-virgin olive oil	1 small red onion, cut into 8 wedges
1 (1-lb.) pork tenderloin, trimmed and halved crosswise	2 Bosc pears, cored and cut into 1/2-in.-thick slices
1 tsp. kosher salt, divided	3 tablespoons white balsamic vinegar
1/2 tsp. freshly ground black pepper	1 ounce Gorgonzola cheese, crumbled (about 1/4 cup)

Directions:

1   Preheat the oven to 500 degrees Fahrenheit.

2   Over medium heat in a large ovenproof skillet heat the olive oil. With 3/4 teaspoon salt and pepper sprinkle the pork.

3   Add pork to the skillet and cook for 5 minutes, turning to brown on all sides.

4   Add onion and pears to the skillet, breaking up onion wedges with a spoon. Transfer the skillet in the oven.

5   Bake at 500 degrees Fahrenheit till the onion is tender and an instant-read thermometer inserted in thickest part of pork indicates 140 degrees Fahrenheit, around 8 minutes. Transfer the pork from the skillet and let it cool down for 3 minutes. Cut into slices.

6   Add remaining 1/4 teaspoon of salt and vinegar to the skillet, scraping skillet to loosen browned bits. Place the pork back to the skillet and sprinkle with cheese. *Enjoy!*

PER SERVING Calories:297kcal; Fat:11.3g; Saturated fat:3.2g; Cholesterol:80mg; Carbohydrate:21g; Sugar:13g; Fiber:4g; Protein:26g

SUMPTUOUS MEDITERRANEAN
DINNER RECIPES

Everyone deserves to go home to a delicious dinner after a hard day at work. However, that does not mean you have to spend a lot of money at a restaurant just to enjoy a mouth-watering Mediterranean meal. Bring out your inner kitchen connoisseur and enjoy any of these easy recipes without ruining your weight loss diet in the process.

APPETIZING TUNA

Serves 12 / Prep time: 15 min / Cook time: - min / Total Time: 15 min

Ingredients:

4 (5 oz.) tuna caned in water, drained

5 hard-boiled eggs, chopped

1/2 cup chopped sweet onion

1 stalk celery, chopped

1 1/2 tablespoons dill pickle relish

2 tsps. honey mustard

3/4 cup mayonnaise

1/2 tsp. celery seed

1/2 tsp. seasoned salt

1/2 tsp. ground black pepper

Directions:

1 In a large bowl mix together tuna, eggs, onion, and celery.

2 In a small bowl mix together relish, honey mustard, mayonnaise, celery seed, salt, and pepper.

3 Combine the mix from the small bowl with the mix from the large bowl, stir gently to coat. Serve at room temperature or let it chill till ready to eat. *Enjoy!*

PER SERVING Calories:186kcal; Fat:13.6g; Saturated fat:2.4g; Cholesterol:106mg; Carbohydrate:2g; Sugar:1g; Fiber:0.2g; Protein:13.6g

AVOCADO AND TUNA

Serves 4 / Prep time: 20 min / Cook time: - min / Total Time: 20 min

Ingredients:

1 (12 oz.) tuna caned in water, drained

1 tablespoon mayonnaise

3 green onions, thinly sliced,

plus, additional for garnish

1/2 red bell pepper, chopped

1 dash balsamic vinegar

black pepper to taste

1 pinch garlic salt, or to taste

2 ripe avocados, halved and pitted

Directions:

1   In a bowl mix together tuna, red pepper, green onions, and balsamic vinegar. Season with garlic salt and pepper.

2   With tuna mixture pack the avocado halves. Before serving garnish with green onions and dash of black pepper. *Enjoy!*

PER SERVING Calories:294kcal; Fat:18.2g; Saturated fat:2.8g; Cholesterol:27mg; Carbohydrate:11g; Sugar:1.9g; Fiber:7.4g; Protein:23.9g

CAULIFLOWER AND TUNA

Serves 6 / Prep time: 6 min / Cook time: 39 min / Total Time: 45 min

Ingredients:

1 large or 2 small or medium cauliflowers, broken into small florets	3 tablespoons capers, drained and rinsed
1 (5 oz.) tuna caned in water, drained	3 tablespoons sherry vinegar or champagne vinegar
1/3 cup chopped flat-leaf parsley	6 tablespoons extra-virgin olive oil
1 plump garlic clove, minced or pureed	Salt and freshly ground pepper
1 tablespoon fresh lemon juice	

Directions:

1   In a steaming basket over 1-inch of boiling water place the cauliflower, cover with lid and steam for 1 minute. Remove the lid for 15 seconds, then cover again and continue steaming for 5 – 8 minutes, or till tender. Refresh with cold water, and then drain on paper towels.

2   Break up the tuna fish in a large bowl and add the cauliflower.

3   In a measuring cup or a small bowl, combine together parsley, garlic, lemon juice, capers, vinegar, and olive oil. Season with salt, and pepper.

4   Add to tuna and cauliflower mix and toss together. Marinate for 30 minutes before serving. Serve warm, cold, or at room temperature. *Enjoy!*

PER SERVING Calories:179kcal; Fat:15g; Saturated fat:2g; Cholesterol:7mg; Carbohydrate:3g; Sugar:0g; Fiber:1g; Protein:7g

GRILLED SALMON KEBABS ONE WAY

Serves 4 / Prep time: 10 min / Cook time: 10 min / Total Time: 20 min

Ingredients:

2 tsp. sesame seeds

2 tbsp. chopped fresh oregano

1/4 tsp. crushed red pepper flakes

1 tsp. ground cumin

1-1 /2 pounds skinless wild salmon fillet, cut into 1-inch pieces

2 lemons, very thinly sliced into rounds

extra-virgin (organic) olive oil spray

1 tsp. kosher salt

16 bamboo skewers soaked in water 1 hour

Directions:

5   Spray the greats with oil and the grill on medium heat. Combine sesame seeds, oregano, red pepper flakes, and cumin in a small bowl, mix well. Set aside spice mixture.

6   Onto 8 pairs of parallel skewers treat salmon and folded lemon slices (beginning and ending with salmon), to make 8 kebabs total. Spray the salmon lightly with olive oil and season with salt and reserved spice mixture.

7   Grill the salmon, turning occasionally, till the salmon is opaque throughout, around 8 – 10 minutes. *Enjoy!*

PER SERVING Calories:267kcal; Fat:11g; Saturated fat:2.1g; Cholesterol:94mg; Carbohydrate:7g; Sugar:0g; Fiber:3g; Protein:35g

GRILLED CEDAR PLANK SALMON

Serves 4 / Prep time: 10 min / Cook time: 20 min / Total Time: 30 min

Ingredients:

1 untreated cedar plank	1 tsp. extra-virgin olive oil
1 (1 1/4 lbs.) boneless wild salmon fillet	1 tsp. red wine vinegar
1 lemon, halved	1/4 cup sliced red onion
1 tsp. dried oregano	1/4 cup Kalamata olives, quartered in long strips
3/4 tsp. kosher salt	1/8 tsp. kosher salt
1/8 tsp. black pepper	black pepper, to taste
few sprigs of fresh oregano and thyme (optional)	fresh oregano for garnish
1 cup grape tomatoes, halved	

Directions:

1 Place the cedar plank in water for 1 hour to soak.

2 Slice into thin slices 1/2 of the lemon. Use the remaining juice from 1/2 of the lemon to season salmon, and also add oregano, salt, and pepper. Cover and refrigerate till ready to grill.

3   Combine in a medium bowl tomatoes, olive oil, vinegar, red onion, olives, salt, and pepper.

4   Place on the plank, skin side down, salmon and fresh herbs. Top that whit lemon slices.

5   Leaving the right burners off (so you have indirect heat) heat the grill to medium-high heat. Close the grill cover and allow the grill to get hot.

6   Transfer the planked salmon on direct heat side for 3 – 4 minutes, till the plank start to smoke and become a little charred on the bottom and edges (keep a spray bottle with water by your side in case the edges of plank ignite, check occasionally to make sure this don't happen).

7   After the 3 – 4 minutes have passed, move the planked salmon to the indirect heat side, close the grill cover, and grill for another 12 – 15 minutes based on the thickness, or till the salmon is cooked throughout in the thickest part (use a fork to take a peak)

8   When the salmon is cooked, cover it with tomato mix and serve. *Enjoy!*

PER SERVING Calories:251kcal; Fat:11g; Saturated fat:1.6g; Cholesterol:78mg; Carbohydrate:8g; Sugar:0g; Fiber:2g; Protein:30g

SALMON BURGERS WITH SRIRACHA MAYO

Serves 4 / Prep time: 1h 20 min / Cook time: 10 min / Total Time: 1h 30 min

Ingredients for the spicy Sriracha mayo:

1 tbsp. Sriracha sauce

3 tbsp. light mayonnaise (Hellman's)

Ingredients for the salmon patties:

1 clove garlic, minced

6 tbsp. panko (or gluten-free panko)

1/4 cup red bell pepper, diced

1/4 cup yellow bell pepper, diced

1 pound wild salmon fillet

1 large egg, lightly beaten

1 tsp. fresh lemon juice

1/2 tbsp. reduced sodium soy sauce

1/4 tsp. kosher salt

extra-virgin (organic) olive oil spray

4 cups baby arugula

4 oz. avocado, sliced

Directions:

1   Mix together Sriracha sauce and mayonnaise, set aside.

2   Remove salmon skin, and cut off about 4 oz. piece off.

3   Finely chop it with food processor or chopper. This will help to hold salmon burgers together. Finely chop the remaining salmon using a knife.

4   Combine in a medium bowl salmon with garlic, panko, and bell peppers.

5   Combine in a small bowl egg, lemon juice, soy sauce, and salt. Add to the salmon mix, and toss gently to combine.

94

6   Form 4 burger patties from the mixture and place it in the refrigerator for at least 1 hour. This will help burgers get firm and hold better together while cooking.

7   With cooking spray lightly coat a grill pan or skillet. Over medium-high heat place the pan till hot.

8   Cook the burger patties for 4 – 5 minutes per side, or till cooked through.

9   On each plate place arugula, and top with salmon burgers, 1 tablespoon of mayo and avocado slices. *Enjoy!*

PER SERVING Calories:290kcal; Fat:15g; Saturated fat:4.1g; Cholesterol:78mg; Carbohydrate:2.1g; Sugar:1.2g; Fiber:0.6g; Protein:32.6g

ARUGULA SALMON SALAD

Serves 1 / Prep time: 10 min / Cook time: 10 min / Total Time: 20 min

Ingredients:

1 1/2 cups baby arugula

4 oz. sockeye wild salmon, skin removed

1 tsp. capers, drained

2 tsp. red wine vinegar

1 tsp. extra-virgin olive oil

1 tbsp. (.25 oz.) shaved Parmesan cheese

salt and fresh pepper to taste

Directions:

1   With a little salt and pepper season the wild salmon, and cook for around 10 minutes, either broiled, on the grill, or in a pan lightly sprayed with olive oil. (*See page 138 on how to cook a salmon*)

2   Put arugula on a dish, sprinkle with salt and pepper and cover with salmon and capers. Drizzle vinegar and olive oil on top and finish with fresh shaved Parmesan cheese. *Enjoy!*

PER SERVING Calories:288kcal; Fat:16.1g; Saturated fat:3.1g; Cholesterol:66.4mg; Carbohydrate:11g; Sugar:2g; Fiber:3g; Protein:26g

TILAPIA WITH PEPPERS AND OLIVES

Serves 4 / Prep time: 10 min / Cook time: 10 min / Total Time: 20 min

Ingredients:

2 tbsp. extra-virgin olive oil

4 (6-oz.) tilapia fillets

kosher salt and black pepper

1 onion, thinly sliced

2 red bell peppers, thinly sliced

1/2 cup pitted green olives

1/2 cup fresh flat-leaf parsley, chopped

2 tbsp. fresh lime juice

Directions:

1   Over medium-high heat in a large non-stick skillet heat 1 tablespoon of olive oil.

2   With 1/4 teaspoon, each, salt and pepper season the tilapia and cook till opaque throughout, 4 – 5 minutes per side.

3   In the meantime, over medium-high heat in a second large skillet heat the remaining 1 tablespoon of olive oil.

4   Stirring often, cook the onion and peppers, till tender, 8 – 10 minutes.

5   Stir in parsley, olives, lime juice, and 1/4 teaspoon each salt and pepper into the vegetables. Serve with the tilapia. *Enjoy!*

PER SERVING Calories:276kcal; Fat:13g; Saturated fat:3g; Cholesterol:73mg; Carbohydrate:8g; Sugar:3g; Fiber:3g; Protein:35g

CILANTRO TILAPIA

Serves 4 / Prep time: 5 min / Cook time: 12 min / Total Time: 17 min

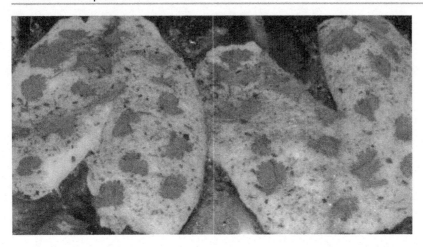

Ingredients:

3 tbsp. extra-virgin olive oil	2 tbsp. Cajun seasoning
4 (4 oz.) tilapia fillets, fresh	black pepper, to taste
2 tbsp. garlic salt	1 bunch cilantro

Directions:

1   Preheat the oven to 375 degrees Fahrenheit.

2   Using olive oil coat the bottom of a baking dish.

3   Arrange tilapia in the pan.

4   Sprinkle garlic salt, Cajun seasoning, and pepper over tilapia fillets.

5   Press a few springs of cilantro on top of each tilapia fillet.

6   Transfer the tilapia into the oven and bake for 8 – 12 minutes. Enjoy alone or with lemon. *Enjoy!*

Tip: Make this into a meal by tossing arugula, baby kale, or other lettuce greens in lemon juice, olive oil, salt and pepper and having as a side salad.

PER SERVING Calories:200.1kcal; Fat:12.1g; Saturated fat:2g; Cholesterol:56.7mg; Carbohydrate:0.3g; Sugar:0.1g; Fiber:0.2g; Protein:22.9g

TILAPIA AL AJILLO

Serves 4 / Prep time: 5 min / Cook time: 15 min / Total Time: 20 min

Ingredients:

1 1/2 lbs. tilapia fillet

4 clove garlic, thinly sliced

3 tbsp. extra-virgin olive oil

salt

pepper

1 lemon, for serving

asparagus

Directions:

7   Use salt and pepper to season tilapia fillets.

8   In a skillet heat olive oil over medium heat.

9   When the olive oil gets hot place tilapia fillets, and when they start to turn color a bit (after 1 – 2 minutes) add garlic slices.

10 Cook for another 4 minutes or so, then flip the fillets.

11 Cook the fillets till cooked through, and the fillets flake easily with a fork (this entirely depends on the thickness of your fillets, so keep a close eye on them).

12 The garlic should get golden brown color, so if you notice that it is starting to burn, spoon it over the fillets, so it is no more in contact with the pan.

13 When fillets are cooked squeeze freshly lemon juice over them.

14 Serve with asparagus and garnish with chopped parsley. *Enjoy!*

PER SERVING Calories:257kcal; Fat:13g; Saturated fat:2g; Cholesterol:85mg; Carbohydrate:1g; Sugar:0g; Fiber:0g; Protein:34g

SAVORY LEMON WHITE FISH FILLET

Serves 4 / Prep time: 15 min / Cook time: 6 min / Total Time: 21 min

Ingredients:

4 (4 to 6 ounces) cod, halibut, or flounder

6 tablespoons extra-virgin olive oil, divided

1/4 teaspoon kosher or sea salt

1/4 teaspoon freshly ground black pepper

2 lemons, one cut in halves, one cut in wedges

Directions:

1   For around 10 -15 minutes allow the fish to sit in a bowl at room temperature.

2   On both side of each fillet rub 1 tablespoon of olive oil and season with salt and pepper.

3   Over medium heat in a skillet or sauté pan add 2 tablespoons of olive oil. After around 1 minute, when the olive oil is hot and simmering, but not smoking add the fillets. Cook for around 2 – 3 minutes per side, so that each side of fillets are browned and cooked through.

4   Squeeze lemon halves over the fillets and remove from the heat. Pour over the fillets any lemon juice if left in the pan. Serve with lemon wedges. *Enjoy!*

Tip: Make this into a meal by tossing arugula, baby kale, or other lettuce greens in lemon juice, olive oil, salt and pepper and having as a side salad.

PER SERVING Calories:197kcal; Fat:12g; Saturated fat:2g; Cholesterol:56mg; Carbohydrate:1g; Sugar:0g; Fiber:0g; Protein:21g

SHRIMP SKEWERS WITH GARLIC-LIME MARINADE

Serves 6 / Prep time: 15 min / Cook time: 5 min / Total Time: 20 min

Ingredients:

1 pound large raw shrimp, cleaned and deveined	1/4 teaspoon paprika
2 tablespoons extra-virgin olive oil	1/4 teaspoon kosher or sea salt
3 cloves garlic, sliced thin	1/4 teaspoon black pepper
1/4 cup fresh squeezed lime juice	1/4 cup finely chopped cilantro or parsley, for serving
	6 large bamboo or metal skewers (if bamboo, soak in warm water 30 minutes prior to cooking)

Directions:

1 For marinade whisk together olive oil, garlic, lemon juice, paprika, salt, and pepper.

2 Threat around 5 – 6 shrimps onto each skewer. Place them on the plate and pour marinade over them.

3 **To grill:** Set the grill to medium heat and oil the grates with olive oil. Place the skewers to the grill and cook for around 2 minutes per side, or till pink and opaque. Drizzle with any extra marinade while cooking.

4 **To roast in oven:** Preheat the oven to 450 degrees Fahrenheit. On the baking sheet place the skewers and roast for around 5 minutes, or till pink and opaque. Garnish with cilantro or parsley before serving, if desired. *Enjoy!*

Tip: Make this into a meal by tossing arugula, baby kale, or other lettuce greens in lemon juice, olive oil, salt and pepper and having as a side salad.

PER SERVING Calories:108kcal; Fat:5g; Saturated fat:1g; Cholesterol:122mg; Carbohydrate:1g; Sugar:0g; Fiber:0g; Protein:15g

GRILLED SALMON KEBOBS OTHER WAY

Ingredients:

1 pound thick wild salmon, without skin, cut into about 12 cubes

Ingredients for the marinade:

2 tablespoons extra-virgin olive oil

2 tablespoons fresh squeezed lemon juice

3 tablespoons minced fresh rosemary

1 tablespoon Dijon mustard

2 cloves garlic, minced

1/2 teaspoon kosher or sea salt

1/2 teaspoon black pepper

4 skewers, if using bamboo or wood soak in warm water for 20 to 30 minutes

Directions:

1   Mix together all the ingredients for marinade.

2   Add salmon to marinade and let it absorb the juices for around 20 minutes at room temperature.

3   Thread pieces of salmon on skewers.

4   Use cooking spray to coat grates of a grill, or a skillet, or a grill pan.

5   Set the heat to high.

6   Once hot, add skewers and cook for around 4 minutes per side, or till the fish is opaque and flakes easily with fork. Drizzle with any leftover marinade while cooking. *Enjoy!*

Tip: Make this into a meal by tossing arugula, baby kale, or other lettuce greens in lemon juice, olive oil, salt and pepper and having as a side salad.

PER SERVING Calories:308kcal; Fat:22g; Saturated fat:5g; Cholesterol:62mg; Carbohydrate:2g; Sugar:0g; Fiber:1g; Protein:24g

LEMON PEPPER SALMON CAESAR SALAD

Serves 8 / Prep time: 20 min / Cook time: 20 min / Total Time: 40 min

Ingredients for the dressing:

1/2 cup plain Greek yogurt

1 teaspoon Dijon mustard

2 tablespoons grated Parmesan cheese

1 garlic clove

2 tablespoons extra-virgin olive oil

1 anchovy filets (optional)

Juice of 1 lemon

Ingredients for the salad:

2 heads Romaine lettuce, chopped

2 ounces Parmesan cheese, shaved with a vegetable peeler

Ingredients for the salmon:

2 teaspoons lemon zest

4 (6 ounce) salmon filets

3/4 teaspoon sea salt

2 tablespoons extra-virgin olive oil

2 teaspoons fresh ground black pepper

Directions:

1   **For the dressing:** In the blender place all the ingredients and pulse till smooth.

2   **For the salad:** In a large bowl add Romaine lettuce and shaved cheese. Mix with dressing till well coated.

3   **For the salmon:** In a small bowl mix together lemon zest, salt, and pepper. Coat salmon fillets with that seasoning. Over medium-high heat place a heavy cast iron or stainless steel skillet. Heat the skillet for 3 – 4 minutes, till very hot, and add olive oil. Add 1 – 2 fillets at a time when olive oil starts to shimmer.

4   The salmon is cooked when it lifts easily with a spatula (if it resists, simply leave it be till it lifts easily). Filip the salmon to another side and continue cooking till it is well-browned on both sides and flakes easily with a fork. Cook the remaining fillets. *Enjoy!*

PER SERVING Calories:323kcal; Fat:22g; Saturated fat:5g; Cholesterol:56mg; Carbohydrate:7g; Sugar:3g; Fiber:4g; Protein:25g

CHICKEN BREASTS WITH MUSHROOM

Serves 4 / Prep time: 10 min / Cook time: 30 min / Total Time: 40 min

Ingredients:

4 boneless, skinless chicken breasts	3 tablespoons olive oil, divided
2 cups baby bella mushrooms	2 tablespoons chopped fresh thyme leaves
1/2 cup diced onions	1 clove garlic, minced
2 tablespoons flour	1/4 teaspoon kosher or sea salt
3/4 cup milk	1/4 teaspoon black pepper

Directions:

1   Pound the chicken breast to an even thickens, using meat tenderizer or bottom of a wide jar.

2   Season each side of chicken breast with salt and pepper.

3   Heat 1 tablespoon of olive oil over medium heat in a sauté pan. When the sauté pan is whole coated with olive oil and hot, add the chicken breasts.

4   Cook the chicken breasts for 1 minute, till golden on the bottom. Flip the breast and lower the heat to low. Cover the pan with a tight fitting lid, and continue cooking for another 10 minutes (do not remove lid while cooking).

5   When the 10 minutes is up, transfer the pan from the heat, still covered, and allow it to sit for an extra 10 minutes.

6   The chicken should be perfectly cooked now, but make sure that there is no pink in the middle of the chicken breast, or that instant-read thermometer registers 165 degrees Fahrenheit in the center of the thickest part of the chicken.

7   Transfer cooked chicken breasts from the pan and set aside (cover to stay warm).

8   Add 1 tablespoon of olive oil to the pan. Increase the heat to medium and add mushrooms and onions.

9   Cook the mushrooms and onions for 5 – 8 minutes, or till the water releases from the mushrooms and evaporates. Add in, whisking, 2 tablespoons of flour and allow to cook for around 1 – 2 minutes, till fragrant.

10   Add the garlic and cook for an extra 30 seconds. Add a 1/4 cup of milk, thyme, salt and pepper. Whisk till thickened. Add another 1/4 cup of milk and whisk till thickened. Repeat this till all of the sauce has thickened.

11   Transfer the chicken breast to a serving plate, pour sauce over it and serve. *Enjoy!*

Tip: Make this into a meal by tossing arugula, baby kale, or other lettuce greens in lemon juice, olive oil, salt and pepper and having as a side salad.

PER SERVING Calories:315kcal; Fat:16g; Saturated fat:3g; Cholesterol:108mg; Carbohydrate:8g; Sugar:4g; Fiber:1g; Protein:35g

CHICKEN AND TOMATO SALAD

Serves 4 / Prep time: 20 min / Cook time: 20 min / Total Time: 40 min

Ingredients:

1/2 lbs. boneless, skinless chicken breast

Salt and freshly ground pepper to taste

1/4 cup extra-virgin olive oil

1 pound fresh, sweet ripe but firm tomatoes, cut in wedges

12 Kalamata olives, pitted and halved

1 small red onion, halved and sliced across the grain

1 tablespoon red wine vinegar or sherry vinegar (more to taste)

1 tablespoon fresh lemon juice

2 oz. feta cheese, crumbled

3 to 4 tablespoons chopped or torn fresh mint leaves (to taste)

1 heart of romaine lettuce, washed, dried and torn

Directions:

1   Preheat the oven to 400 degrees Fahrenheit.

2   With salt and pepper season the chicken breasts. Place them in a bowl and coat them with 2 tablespoon of olive oil.

3   Heat, over high heat, grill pan or a cast iron pan.

4   Sear the chicken breasts for around 2 minutes per side, till grill marks show up if using a grill pan, or till nicely browned if using a cast iron pan.

5   Place seared chicken breasts to a baking sheet and place in the oven. Roast for 10 – 15 minutes, or till an instant-read thermometer registers 165 degrees Fahrenheit in the center of the thickest part of the chicken. Remove from the oven and let it cool down.

6   In the meantime, put the sliced onion in a bowl and cover with water. Soak for 5 minutes, drain and rinse well.

7   When the chicken has cooled down enough so it can be handled, tear it into bite-size pieces and put in a bowl.

8   Add in tomatoes, olives, and onion. Season with salt and pepper. Toss with the remaining olive oil, vinegar, and lemon juice. Add in feta and mint and toss again.

9   Serve in wide salad bowl with lettuce. Cover with the chicken and tomato salad. *Enjoy!*

PER SERVING Calories:278kcal; Fat:19g; Saturated fat:4g; Cholesterol:54mg; Carbohydrate:10g; Sugar:5g; Fiber:3g; Protein:17g

CHICKEN WITH LEMON AND HERBS

Serves 6 / Prep time: 10 min / Cook time: 35 min / Total Time: 45 min

Ingredients:

1 lbs. boneless, skinless chicken breast, four 4 oz. halves

1/2 tsp. sea salt

1/4 tsp. black pepper, freshly ground

1 tsp. extra-virgin olive oil

2 tsp. fresh lemon juice, or to taste

2 tsp. fresh rosemary, chopped

2 tsp. fresh parsley, chopped

1/4 cup chicken broth

1 medium lemon, quartered, for garnish (optional)

Directions:

10 Preheat the oven to 400 degrees Fahrenheit.

11   Season the chicken with salt and pepper, both sides. Transfer to a small, shallow roasting pan and drizzle with olive oil. Sprinkle with lemon juice and garnish with rosemary and parsley. Around the chicken pour broth to coat the bottom of the roasting pan.

12   Place roasting pan in the oven and bake for 30 – 35 minutes, or till the chicken is cooked through. Garnish with fresh lemon, if desired, and serve. *Enjoy!*

Tip: Make this into a meal by tossing arugula, baby kale, or other lettuce greens in lemon juice, olive oil, salt and pepper and having as a side salad.

PER SERVING Calories:146kcal; Fat:4g; Saturated fat:1g; Cholesterol:73mg; Carbohydrate:1g; Sugar:0g; Fiber:0g; Protein:25g

CHICKEN ROLLATINI

Serves 4 / Prep time: 10 min / Cook time: 25 min / Total Time: 35 min

Ingredients:

8 thin sliced boneless skinless chicken cutlets, 3 oz. each

1/2 cup sun dried tomato bruschetta

1/2 cup part-skim shredded mozzarella

1/2 cup chopped baby spinach

1/4 small red onion, sliced

1/2 cup seasoned breadcrumbs

1/4 cup grated Pecorino Romano cheese (or parmesan)

1 lemon, juice of

1 tbsp. extra-virgin olive oil

extra-virgin (organic) olive oil non-stick spray

Directions:

1   Preheat the oven to 450 degrees Fahrenheit.

2   In a shallow bowl combine bread crumbs and grated cheese.

3   In another bowl combine olive oil, lemon juice, and pepper.

4   With non-stick spray lightly spray a 9 x 12-inch baking dish.

5   Place each chicken cutlet on a cutting board and spread, on each of them, 1 tablespoon mozzarella cheese, 1 tablespoon sun-dried tomato bruschetta, 2 – 3 slices red onion, and 1 tablespoon spinach leaves in the center. Roll the chicken cutlets and place them, seam-side down, on a working surface.

6   When finished rolling, dip the rolled chicken cutlets into the lemon-oil mix, then into the bread crumbs mix and place them onto a baking sheet.

7   Spray the top of the rolled chicken cutlets with olive oil spray and bake for 25 minutes, till golden and cooked through. *Enjoy!*

PER SERVING Calories:267kcal; Fat:14g; Saturated fat:4g; Cholesterol:68mg; Carbohydrate:10g; Sugar:4g; Fiber:1.5g; Protein:25g

CHICKEN WITH OLIVES AND HERBS

Serves 4 / Prep time: 10 min / Cook time: 16 min / Total Time: 26 min

Ingredients:

1/2 tbsp. extra-virgin olive oil

4 (8 oz.) boneless chicken breasts

1/2 tsp kosher salt

2 tsps. all purpose or gluten free flour

1/2 cup dry white wine

1/4 cup lemon juice

2 cloves garlic, crushed

1 tsp. chopped fresh thyme

1 cup pitted chopped olives

1 tbsp. chopped fresh parsley

4 thin lemon slices (optional)

Directions:

8   Preheat the oven to 400 degrees Fahrenheit with center positioned rack.

9   Over medium-high heat in a 10-inch cast iron skillet heat the olive oil. Season the chicken with salt and pepper and sprinkle with flour.

10   Sear chicken when olive oil become hot, sear for around 3 minutes per side.

11   Add in wine, lemon juice, garlic, thyme, and olives. Top with lemon slices, if desired.

12   Move the pan to the preheated oven and bake around 10 minutes, until an instant-read thermometer registers 165 degrees Fahrenheit in the center of the thickest part of the chicken.

13   Serve hot topped with parsley. *Enjoy!*

PER SERVING Calories:351kcal; Fat:11g; Saturated fat:3g; Cholesterol:166mg; Carbohydrate:4.5g; Sugar:0.5g; Fiber:1g; Protein:52.5g

CHICKEN AND VEGGIE DINNER

Serves 7 / Prep time: 15 min / Cook time: 30 min / Total Time: 45 min

Ingredients for the seasoning:

1 tsp. kosher salt	1/8 tsp. black pepper
1/2 tsp. onion powder	1 clove crushed garlic
1/2 tsp. dried oregano	3 tbsp. extra-virgin olive oil
1/2 tsp. dried basil	2 tbsp. red wine vinegar
1/4 tsp. thyme	

Ingredients for the sheet pan:

extra-virgin (organic) olive oil spray	1 yellow bell pepper, cut into 1-inch pieces
8 (4 oz. each) boneless skinless chicken thighs, trimmed of fat	12 oz. zucchini, diced into 1-inch pieces
1/2 tsp. kosher salt	1 red onion, cut into 1-inch pieces
3 carrots, peeled and diced into 1-inch pieces	chopped parsley for garnish
1 red bell pepper, cut into 1-inch pieces	

Directions:

1   Preheat the oven to 450 degrees Fahrenheit.

2   Use parchment paper or foil (for easy cleanup) or spray 2 large non-stick sheet pans with olive oil.

3   In a large bowl combine the Italian seasoning. Season the chicken with 1/2 teaspoon salt. After that add the chicken, carrots, bell peppers, zucchini, and red onion to the bowl

and toss to coat. Marinate at least for 30 minutes or as long as overnight.

4   In a single layer spread out everything onto the prepared baking sheets. Chicken and vegetables should not touch. Bake for around 20 minutes, turn the chicken and vegetables and continue baking for another 10 minutes, till roasted and tender. Cover with fresh parsley and serve. *Enjoy!*

PER SERVING Calories:429kcal; Fat:20g; Saturated fat:4g; Cholesterol:214mg; Carbohydrate:15.5g; Sugar:4.5g; Fiber:4g; Protein:46.5g

SUPERB CHICKEN SALAD

Serves 4 / Prep time: 15 min / Cook time: 15 min / Total Time: 30 min

Ingredients:

extra-virgin (organic) olive oil spray	16 oz. (2 large) skinless boneless chicken breasts, cut into 24 1-inch chunks
2 tsp. extra-virgin olive oil	kosher salt and pepper to taste
6 tbsp. whole wheat Italian seasoned breadcrumbs	4 cups shredded romaine
2 tbsp. panko	1 cup shredded red cabbage

Ingredients for the sauce:

2 1/2 tbsp. light mayonnaise	1 1/2 tbsp. Sweet Chili Sauce
2 tbsp. scallions, chopped fine plus more for topping	1 tablespoon Sriracha (or to taste)

Directions:

1 Preheat the oven to 425 degrees Fahrenheit.

2 With olive oil spray coat a baking sheet.

3 In one bowl put the olive oil and in another bowl put breadcrumbs and panko.

4   With salt and pepper season the chicken. Place the chicken in to the olive oil bowl and mix well so the chicken is evenly coated with olive oil.

5   Put chicken breasts, one at a time, into the breadcrumb mix to coat, then arrange evenly on the baking sheet.

6   With olive oil spray lightly spray the top of coated chicken breasts.

7   Bake for 8 – 10 minutes. Turn them over and continue to cook another 4 – 5 minutes or till cook through.

8   In the meantime, in a medium bowl combine the sauce. When the chicken is done, drizzle it over the top and serve. *Enjoy!*

PER SERVING Calories:245kcal; Fat:8g; Saturated fat:2.3g; Cholesterol:86mg; Carbohydrate:13g; Sugar:3g; Fiber:2g; Protein:29g

BREADED CHICKEN CUTLETS

Serves 4 / Prep time: 15 min / Cook time: 15 min / Total Time: 30 min

Ingredients for the chicken:

2 (8 oz.) boneless chicken breasts, cut in half lengthwise

1/4 tsp. salt

2 large egg whites, beaten

1/2 tsp. Sazon seasoning (homemade or packaged)

1/2 cup seasoned breadcrumbs

1 -1/2 tbsp. extra-virgin olive oil

Ingredients for the guacamole:

4 oz. avocado (from 1 small Hass)

1 cup grape tomatoes, halved

1/4 cup slivered red onion

1/4 cup cilantro leaves

1/4 tsp. kosher salt and black pepper

1/4 tsp. cumin

juice of 1/2 lime

4 lime wedges for serving

1   Sprinkle cutlets with Sazon seasoning. In a shallow bowl place bread crumbs. I a different bowl beat egg whites and Sazon together.

2   Dip the chicken in egg whites, after that in bread crumb mix, shaking off excess.

3   Place a large non-stick frying pan over medium heat and add the olive oil.

4   Add the chicken cutlets when olive oil gets hot and cook around 6 minutes per side, till golden brown and cooked through.

5   Combine in a large bowl the avocado, tomato, red onion, cumin, lime juice, salt, and pepper. Lightly toss and serve over the chicken cutlets with additional lime wedges. *Enjoy!*

PER SERVING Calories:286kcal; Fat:13g; Saturated fat:2g; Cholesterol:83mg; Carbohydrate:12g; Sugar:1g; Fiber:3g; Protein:31g

CHICKEN AND TOMATO KEBABS

Serves 8 / Prep time: 3 h / Cook time: 6 min / Total Time: 3 h 6 min

Ingredients:

1 cup fresh basil leaves, chopped

1/4 cup grated Parmigiano Reggiano cheese

1 clove garlic

kosher salt and fresh pepper to taste

3 tbsp. extra-virgin olive oil

1-1/4 lbs. skinless chicken breast, cut into 1-inch cubes

24 cherry tomatoes

16 wooden skewers (or use metal ones), soak in water at least 30 minutes

Directions:

1   Pulse in a food processor till smooth basil, Parmesan cheese, garlic, salt, and pepper. While pulsing slowly add the olive oil.

2   Combine in a bowl pesto with the raw chicken and marinate for at least 2 hours. Thread chicken and tomatoes onto 8 pairs of parallel skewers (beginning and ending with chicken) to make 8 kebabs total.

3   Heat over the medium-high heat outdoor grill or indoor grill pan. Make sure that the grates are clean and spray them lightly with olive oil.

4   Transfer the chicken onto the hot grill and cook for around 3 – 4 minutes. Flip and cook till the chicken is cooked through, around 2 – 3 minutes more. *Enjoy!*

PER SERVING Calories:147kcal; Fat:7.5g; Saturated fat:3.2g; Cholesterol:2.5mg; Carbohydrate:3g; Sugar:0g; Fiber:1g; Protein:18g

CHICKEN WITH GARLIC YOGURT SAUCE

Serves 4 / Prep time: 60 min / Cook time: 15 min / Total Time: 75 min

Ingredients for the chicken:

1 lbs. (2) boneless, skinless chicken breasts, cut in half lengthwise

1 tbsp. extra-virgin olive oil

juice from 1 medium lemon

3 garlic cloves, minced

1 tsp. smoked paprika

1/4 tsp. curry powder

1 tsp. cumin

1/4 tsp. turmeric

pinch red pepper flakes

1/8 tsp. cinnamon

1 tsp. kosher salt

freshly ground black pepper, to taste

Ingredients for the garlic yogurt sauce:

1 (7 oz.) container 2% Greek yogurt

2 tbsp. lemon juice

2 garlic cloves, finely minced

1/8 tbsp. kosher salt

chopped parsley (for garnish)

Directions:

1   In a Ziploc bag, one at a time, place the chicken breast. Using a meat tenderizer pound chicken breasts to an even thickness, around 1/2-inch thick (careful not to rupture the bag). Take all the pounded chicken breasts and place them back into the Ziploc bag and set it aside.

2   Combine the olive oil and lemon juice in a medium bowl and whisk till well combined. Add the garlic, paprika, curry powder, cumin, turmeric, red pepper, cinnamon, salt, and pepper and whisk again.

3   Pour the marinade into the Ziploc bag where the pounded chicken is. Massage it to evenly coat. Let it marinate in a refrigerator for at least 1 hour, or even overnight.

4   Combine in a small bowl the yogurt, garlic, lemon juice, and salt. Mix to combine well and refrigerate till ready to use.

5   Grill the chicken over medium-high heat for 3 minutes, or till it no longer sticks to the grill. Flip the chicken and grill an extra 3 – 4 minutes.

6   Allow the chicken to cool down for 5 minutes before slicing it. Before serving, cover each chicken breast with 2 tablespoons of sauce and a sprinkle of parsley. *Enjoy!*

PER SERVING Calories:240kcal; Fat:11g; Saturated fat:2.5g; Cholesterol:75mg; Carbohydrate:5g; Sugar:2g; Fiber:0.5g; Protein:30g

GREEK FETA-ZUCCHINI TURKEY BURGERS

Serves 5 / Prep time: 20 min / Cook time: 10 min / Total Time: 30 min

Ingredients:

1 lbs. 93% lean ground turkey

1/4 cup seasoned whole wheat breadcrumbs

5 oz. grated zucchini (when squeezed 4 oz.)

2 tbsp. grated red onion

1 clove garlic, crushed

1 tbsp. fresh oregano

3/4 tsp kosher salt and fresh pepper

1/4 cup crumbled feta cheese (from Salad Savors)

extra-virgin (organic) olive oil spray

Ingredients for the salad:

1 cucumber, diced

3/4 cup quartered grape tomatoes

2 tbsp. chopped red onion

1/3 cup Kalamata olives

1/4 cup roasted peppers

2 tsp. red wine vinegar

1 tsp. fresh oregano

1 tsp. extra-virgin olive oil

kosher salt

1 tbsp. crumbled feta

Directions:

1   Using paper towels squeeze all the moisture from the zucchini.

2   Combine in a large bowl, mixing well, ground turkey, bread crumbs, zucchini, onion, garlic, oregano, salt, and pepper. Add in 1/4 cup of feta cheese, mix well, and make 5 equally sized patties (not to thick so they can easily be cooked in the center).

3   Combine in a medium bowl, mixing well, the tomato, cucumber, vinegar, red onion, salt and remaining Feta.

4   **If cooking indoors:** Heat, over medium-high heat, large non-stick skillet. Lightly spray olive oil when the skillet is hot. Transfer the burgers to the pan and lower the heat to low. Cook till browned then flip. Flip over a couple of times to prevent the burgers from burning and also to make sure they are cooked all the way through.

5   **If grilling:** Before cooking clean the grill and then generously oil the grates to prevent sticking. On medium heat cook the burgers around 5 minutes per side, or till no longer pink in the center.

6   Transfer the burgers on a dish and top with 2/3 of salad and serve. *Enjoy!*

PER SERVING Calories:221kcal; Fat:11g; Saturated fat:3g; Cholesterol:73mg; Carbohydrate:10g; Sugar:1g; Fiber:2g; Protein:20g

EASY MEDITERRANEAN
SNACK RECIPES

If you are craving for a tasty snack in between meals, you no longer have to eat those unhealthy chips or that fattening slab of cake. Here are some Mediterranean snack and dessert recipes that are easy and fun to make!

CRISPY LENTIL ENERGY BITES

Serves 21 / Prep time: 40 min / Cook time: 30 min / Total Time: 1 h 10 min

Ingredients:

1/2 cup dry green lentils

1/2 tbsp. extra-virgin coconut oil, melted

1 tsp cinnamon

1 tsp coconut flour

1/8 tsp sea salt

2 cups dry quick oats

1/4 cup unsweetened coconut, shredded

1/4 cup pumpkin seeds

1/4 organic dark chocolate chips (70% cacao or higher)

1/2 cup organic peanut butter

1/2 cup honey or maple syrup (or a combo of both)

Directions:

1　Preheat your oven to 400 degrees Fahrenheit and line a baking sheet with parchment paper.

2　Rinse lentils and transfer them to a small saucepan. Cover them with 2 cups of water and bring to a boil. Lower heat to medium and simmer for 15 minutes.

3　Drain lentils and transfer them to a small mixing bowl. Stir in the coconut oil and coat the lentils. Sprinkle with cinnamon, coconut flour and sea salt and stir well.

4　Spread lentils evenly onto lined baking sheet and bake for 15 minutes, stirring after halfway and keep an eye on them if they start to burn.

5　Set the lentils aside to cool.

6　Meanwhile, in a large mixing bowl, stir together the oats, seeds, coconut and chocolate chips. Add in crispy lentils, then the peanut butter and honey/maple syrup and stir well again.

7   Roll into tablespoon sized balls and refrigerate for 30 minutes

8   Store covered in the fridge or freezer. *Enjoy!*

PER SERVING Calories:162kcal; Fat:6.2g; Saturated fat:1.9g; Cholesterol:0mg; Carbohydrate:22.6g; Sugar:4g; Fiber:2.9g; Protein:5.8g

ZESTY BLACK BEAN HUMMUS

Serves 8 / Prep time: 5 min / Cook time: - min / Total Time: 5 min

Ingredients:

2 (15.5 ounce) cans black beans

2 cups low-fat cottage cheese

3 tablespoons almond butter

1 garlic clove, sliced

2 tablespoons extra-virgin olive oil

3 tablespoons red wine vinegar

3/4 teaspoon sea salt

1/2 teaspoon ground cumin

1 teaspoon ground coriander

1/4 cup fresh parsley

2 tablespoons orange zest

Freshly ground black pepper to taste

10-12 stalks of celery, cut into thirds

Directions:

1   Mix all the ingredients in a food processor, except celery, and puree till smooth. If necessary, scrap down the sides.

2   Move to a bowl and serve with celery. *Enjoy!*

PER SERVING Calories:218kcal; Fat:7.5g; Saturated fat:1.5g; Cholesterol:10mg; Carbohydrate:20g; Sugar:4.5g; Fiber:5.5g; Protein:16g

ROASTED CHICKPEAS

Serves 2 / Prep time: 25 min / Cook time: 30 min / Total Time: 55 min

Ingredients:

1 can chickpeas	1/2 teaspoon dried basil
1 teaspoon extra-virgin olive oil	1 teaspoon Nutritional Yeast (or Parmesan)
1/4 teaspoon salt	1/4 teaspoon red pepper flakes
1/2 teaspoon garlic powder	1/2 teaspoon dried basil

Directions:

1   Preheat the oven to 450 degrees Fahrenheit.

2   Rinse and drain the chickpeas, pat them dry after.

3   Combine in a small mixing bowl chickpeas, olive oil and seasoning. Mix well.

4   Cover the baking pan with aluminum foil and pour chickpeas onto it. Gently shake the chickpeas till they are all in one layer.

5   Roast the chickpeas in the oven for 10 – 15 minutes, toss, and roast for another 10 – 15 minutes till they are golden and starting to brown (this will make them even more crispier). Serve as a snack or toss into a salad. *Enjoy!*

PER SERVING Calories:395kcal; Fat:8.5g; Saturated fat:1.5g; Cholesterol:2mg; Carbohydrate:60.5g; Sugar:10.5g; Fiber:17.5g; Protein:20.5g

PORTOBELLO MUSHROOM DELIGHT

Serves 2 / Prep time: 5 min / Cook time: 15 min / Total Time: 20 min

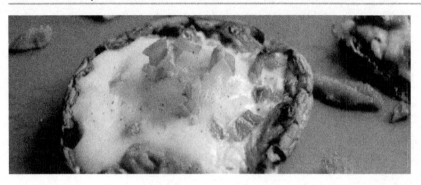

Ingredients:

2 Portobello mushroom caps (around 3 ounces each)

2 tablespoons soft goat cheese

2 tablespoons sundried tomatoes

2 large eggs

extra-virgin (organic) olive oil spray

Salt and pepper to taste

Basil for garnish

Directions:

1   Preheat the oven to 400 degrees Fahrenheit.

2   From the mushroom caps remove the stems and with a spoon scrape out the gills.

3   Use cooking spray to spray both sides of the mushroom and set them onto the baking sheet.

4   Place into each mushroom 1 tablespoon of goat cheese, where the gills used to be.

5   Finely chop sun-dried tomatoes and sprinkle into each mushroom cap 1 tablespoon of them.

6   Into each mushroom cap crack an egg, striving to get the yolk to sit in the cavity where the steam was, so it doesn't move around.

7   Transfer the baking sheet to the oven and bake for 15 minutes.

8   Once the eggs are done to your liking, transfer them from the oven and season with salt and pepper.

9   Top with sliced basil and serve. *Enjoy!*

Tip: Make this into a meal by tossing arugula, baby kale, or other lettuce greens in lemon juice, olive oil, salt and pepper and having as a side salad.

PER SERVING Calories:122kcal; Fat:8.5g; Saturated fat:3g; Cholesterol:223mg; Carbohydrate:2g; Sugar:1g; Fiber:0.5g; Protein:8.5g

GREEK PEANUT BUTTER YOGURT

Serves 1 / Prep time: 5 min / Cook time: - min / Total Time: 5 min

Ingredients:

6 oz. plain Greek Yogurt (Chobani)   1 tbsp. natural peanut butter

4 tsp reduced sugar grape jelly   1/8 cup unsalted peanuts

2 tbsp. red seedless grapes, cut in half

Directions:

Place the Greek yogurt in a bowl. Cover with jelly and peanut butter. Sprinkle peanuts and grapes and serve. *Enjoy!*

PER SERVING Calories:359kcal; Fat:17.1g; Saturated fat:0g; Cholesterol:2mg; Carbohydrate:22.4g; Sugar:16.6g; Fiber:2.7g; Protein:27.9g

TUNA SALAD ON CRACKERS

Serves 4 / Prep time: 10 min / Cook time: - min / Total Time: 10 min

Ingredients:

1 (7 ounce) can Albacore Tuna in brine water

2 tablespoons celery, finely chopped

3 tablespoons Canola Oil Mayonnaise

1/2 teaspoon lemon pepper

11/2 tablespoons red onion, finely chopped

1/4 teaspoon dried dill weed

16 Ritz Crackers

2 green leaf lettuce leaves, torn

Fresh dill, for garnish (optional)

Directions:

1   In a mixing bowl place tuna and mash up to desired size pieces. Add in celery, mayonnaise, lemon pepper, onion, and dill weed. Mix well to combine.

2   On top of each cracker place a piece of torn lettuce and top that with 1 tablespoon of tuna salad. Decorate with a piece of fresh dill weed, if desired and serve. *Enjoy!*

PER SERVING (4 crackers) Calories:165kcal; Fat:7g; Saturated fat:1g; Cholesterol:19mg; Carbohydrate:9g; Sugar:1g; Fiber:1g; Protein:13g

HARDBOILED EGG AND AVOCADO BOWL

Serves 1 / Prep time: 5 min / Cook time: 12 min / Total Time: 17 min

Ingredients:

2 hardboiled eggs, chopped	1 heaping Tablespoon red onion, finely chopped
1 teaspoon aluminum free baking soda	1/4 cup red bell pepper, finely chopped
1/2 large avocado, chopped	sea salt and ground pepper, to taste

Directions:

1   At the bottom of a saucepan place the eggs in a single layer. Cover the eggs with water. Add in baking soda (it will help in easily removing egg shell).

2   Bring the water to a full boil by placing the pan on a high heat. Turn the heat off but keep the pan on the hot burner.

3   Cover the pan with the lid and let it sit for 12 – 12 minutes. With cold water cool the eggs. Remove shell from the eggs and slice them into small-size pieces.

4   Mix together in a bowl eggs, avocado, onion, and bell pepper. Season with salt and pepper and serve. *Enjoy!*

PER SERVING Calories:246kcal; Fat:17.6g; Saturated fat:4.7g; Cholesterol:373mg; Carbohydrate:8g; Sugar:3.1g; Fiber:4.2g; Protein:13.4g

CHIPOTLE LIME EDAMAME

Serves 1 / Prep time: 5 min / Cook time: 5 min / Total Time: 10 min

Ingredients

1 cup package frozen shelled edamame	1/4 teaspoon salt
1 tablespoon lime juice	1/4 teaspoon pepper
1/4 teaspoon chipotle powder	2 tablespoons sunflower seeds

Directions:

1. According to the package instructions cook the edamame.

2. In a small bowl, mix together lime juice, chipotle powder, salt, and pepper.

3. To the edamame mixture add the lime juice and toss to coat.

4. Before serving mix in the sunflower seeds. *Enjoy!*

PER SERVING Calories:232kcal; Fat:15g; Saturated fat:1g; Cholesterol:0mg; Carbohydrate:16g; Sugar:3.5g; Fiber:8g; Protein:16g

MEDITERRANEAN PICNIC SNACK

Serves 1 / Prep time: 5 min / Cook time: - min / Total Time: 5 min

Ingredients

1 slice crusty whole-wheat bread, cut
into bite-size pieces

10 cherry tomatoes

1/4 ounce sliced aged cheese

6 oil-cured olives

Directions:

Mix together bread pieces, tomatoes, cheese and olives in a portable container. *Enjoy!*

PER SERVING Calories:197kcal; Fat:9g; Saturated fat:2g; Cholesterol:5mg;
Carbohydrate:22g; Sugar:6g; Fiber:4g; Protein:7g

TOMATO-BASIL SKEWERS

Serves 16 / Prep time: 10 min / Cook time: - min / Total Time: 10 min

Ingredients

16 small fresh mozzarella balls

16 fresh basil leaves

16 cherry tomatoes

Extra-virgin olive oil, to drizzle

Directions:

1   On small skewers, thread mozzarella, basil, and tomatoes.

2   Drizzle with olive oil and season with salt and pepper. *Enjoy!*

PER SERVING Calories:46kcal; Fat:3g; Saturated fat:2g; Cholesterol:8mg; Carbohydrate:1g; Sugar:0g; Fiber:0g; Protein:3g

HEAVENLY MEDITERRANEAN
DESSERT RECIPES

GREEK BAKLAVA

Serves 18 / Prep time: 15 min / Cook time: 50 min / Total Time: 1 h 5 min

Ingredients:

1 (16 oz.) package phyllo dough	1 cup water
1 pound chopped nuts	1 cup white sugar
1 cup butter	1 tsp. vanilla extract
1 tsp. ground cinnamon	1/2 cup honey

Directions:

1 Preheat the oven to a 350 degrees Fahrenheit. Use the 9x13 inch pan and butter the bottoms and the sides.

2 Chop nuts and mix in the cinnamon. Set aside. Unroll phyllo dough. To fit in the pan cut whole stack in half. To keep from drying out as you work use dampened cloth to cover phyllo dough.

3 In the pan place to sheets of phyllo dough and butter thoroughly. Repeat this process until you have 8 sheets layered. On the top sprinkle 2 – 3 tablespoon of nut and cinnamon mix. Cover with 2 sheets of dough, butter, nuts, layering as you move on. The last, top, layer should be around 6 – 8 sheets deep.

4 Cut by using a sharp knife diamond or square shapes all through to the bottom of the pan. To make diagonal cuts you can cut into 4 long rows. In about 50 minutes of baking baklava will be golden and crispy.

5 While baklava is baking prepare the sauce. Put sugar in the boiling water and stir until the sugar is melted. Add vanilla extract and honey. Simmer for about 20 minutes.

6 Take baklava out from the oven and immediately spoon sauce over it. Let it cool down. For serving use cupcake papers. This freezes well. It will get soggy if it's wrapped up so best leave it uncovered. *Enjoy!*

PER SERVING Calories:393kcal; Fat:25.9g; Saturated fat:9g; Cholesterol:27mg; Carbohydrate:37.5g; Sugar:19.9g; Fiber:13.1g; Protein:6.1g

PUMPKIN PIE SMOOTHIE

Serves 2 / Prep time: 5 min / Cook time: - min / Total Time: 5 min

Ingredients:

8 ice cubes, or as desired

1 banana

1/4 cup yogurt

1/4 cup pumpkin puree

1/8 tsp. ground cinnamon

1 pinch ground ginger

Directions:

Mix banana, pumpkin, yogurt, cinnamon, ginger, and ice cubes together in a blender till smooth. *Enjoy!*

PER SERVING Calories:84kcal; Fat:0.8g; Saturated fat:0.4g; Cholesterol:2mg; Carbohydrate:18.6g; Sugar:10.4g; Fiber:2.6g; Protein:2.6g

KEY LIME PIE

Serves 8 / Prep time: 5 min / Cook time: - min / Total Time: 2 h 5 min

Ingredients:

1 reduced fat graham cracker crust

1 (1/16 oz.) package sugar-free lime gelatin

1/4 cup boiling water

1 (8 oz.) container fat-free whipped topping

2 (6 oz.) key lime pie yogurt

Directions:

1 Bring water to a boil.

2 In a large mixing bowl add gelatin powder and pour in boiling water. Dissolve gelatin by using wire whisk.

3 Stir in the yogurt using a wire whisk.

4 Fold in whipped topping with a wooden spoon.

5 Spread on the cracker crust.

6 Refrigerate for a minimum of 2 hours. *Enjoy!*

PER SERVING Calories:42.6kcal; Fat:1.4g; Saturated fat:0.8g; Cholesterol:4.5mg; Carbohydrate:7.1g; Sugar:4.5g; Fiber:0.1g; Protein:0.9g

CHOCOLATE CUPCAKES

Serves 18 / Prep time: 10 min / Cook time: 35 min / Total Time: 45 min

Ingredients:

1 (15 oz.) can pumpkin

18 ounces devil's food cake mix

1/4-1/2 cup water

Directions:

1   Preheat the oven to a 350 degrees Fahrenheit.

2   Combine all the ingredients together by using a mixer.

3   Bake in mini muffin tins for 30 – 35 minutes. *Enjoy!*

PER SERVING Calories:127.7kcal; Fat:4.5g; Saturated fat:0.9g; Cholesterol:0mg; Carbohydrate:22.3g; Sugar:11.2g; Fiber:0.8g; Protein:1.9g

EASY TASTY FROZEN PIE

Serves 8 / Prep time: 5 min / Cook time: - min / Total Time: 5 min

Ingredients:

1 (8 oz.) container fat-free cool whip

1 (6 oz.) container light yogurt

Directions:

Combine the two ingredients and pour them into the pie plate and freeze. *Enjoy!*

PER SERVING Calories:13.1kcal; Fat:0.7g; Saturated fat:0.5g; Cholesterol:2.8mg; Carbohydrate:1g; Sugar:1g; Fiber:0g; Protein:0.7g

ICE CREAM SANDWICH

Serves 1 / Prep time: 1 min / Cook time: - min / Total Time: 1 min

Ingredients:

1 whole honey graham crackers

1 tablespoon light whipped cream

Directions:

1 Crack in half graham crackers.

2 Put on one-half of the cracker 1 tablespoon of whipped

3 cream and cover it with another half of the cracker.

4 Press softly and put in the freezer till ready to be eaten. *Enjoy!*

PER SERVING Calories:37.3kcal; Fat:1.4g; Saturated fat:0.5g; Cholesterol:2.3mg; Carbohydrate:5.8g; Sugar:2.4g; Fiber:0.2g; Protein:0.6g

CARAMEL APPLE FLUFF

Serves 10 / Prep time: 5 min / Cook time: - min / Total Time: 2 h 5 min

Ingredients:

8 oz. crushed pineapple (undrained)

1 oz. sugar-free fat-free butterscotch pudding (small box)

4 apples, chopped

12 oz. fat-free cool whip

Directions:

1   Combine pineapple and dry pudding

2   Add cool whip and apples.

3   Refrigerate for around 2 hours before serving. *Enjoy!*

PER SERVING Calories:51.5kcal; Fat:0.1g; Saturated fat:0g; Cholesterol:0mg; Carbohydrate:13.3g; Sugar:10.8g; Fiber:1.9g; Protein:0.3g

PUMPKIN CUPCAKES

Serves 24 / Prep time: 10 min / Cook time: 25 min / Total Time: 35 min

Ingredients:

1 (18 oz.) box spice cake mix

1 cup water

15 oz. canned pumpkin

1 tsp. vanilla extract

1 12 tsp. cinnamon

Directions:

1   Preheat the oven to a 350 degrees Fahrenheit.

2   Line 24 cupcake pans. Combine all the ingredients in bowl and pour into the cupcake pans.

3   Transfer to the oven and bake for 25 minutes.

4   Cool on cooling rack. They are very moist cupcakes. *Enjoy!*

PER SERVING Calories:100.2kcal; Fat:3g; Saturated fat:0.8g; Cholesterol:0mg; Carbohydrate:17.5g; Sugar:10.6g; Fiber:1g; Protein:1.1g

PINK FLUFF

Serves 10 / Prep time: 1 h / Cook time: - min / Total Time: 1 h

Ingredients:

20 oz. light cherry pie filling

6 oz. Del Monte crushed pineapple in 100% juice

8 oz. Cool Whip Free

1 oz. fat-free sugar-free white chocolate pudding mix

Directions:

1   Combine the pudding straight from the envelope with the cool whip.

2   Empty Del Monte crushed pineapple juice into cherry pie filling.

3   Combine the pie filling with the cool whip and let it cool down in the refrigerator for 1 hour. *Enjoy!*

PER SERVING Calories:50.3kcal; Fat:1g; Saturated fat:0.1g; Cholesterol:0mg; Carbohydrate:11.8g; Sugar:9.6g; Fiber:1g; Protein:0.7g

YOGURT FLUFF

Serves 10 / Prep time: 5 min / Cook time: - min / Total Time: 35 min

Ingredients:

3/4 cup boiling water

1 (3 oz.) package cherry Jell-O (sugar free)

Ice cube

1/2 cup cold water

1 cup plain nonfat yogurt

1/2 tsp. vanilla

Directions:

1   Use a medium size mixing bowl to stir in boiling water into gelatin powder for at least 2 minutes, or till completely dissolved.

2   Add in a sufficient number of ice cubes to cold water to measure 1 cup. Add to Jell-O and stir till slightly thickened. Take away any un-melted ice.

3   Add vanilla and yogurt and stir using wire whisk till blended well. Pure equally into 4 dessert dishes.

4   Refrigerate for 30 minutes or till firm. Before serving add dollop of whipped cream. *Enjoy!*

PER SERVING Calories:35.3kcal; Fat:0.1g; Saturated fat:0.1g; Cholesterol:1.2mg; Carbohydrate:4.8g; Sugar:4.8g; Fiber:0g; Protein:3.5g

PART THREE
QUICK NUTRITIONAL REFERENCE TABLE

Breakfast

Page	Meal	Fat (grams)	Carbs (grams)	Protein (grams)	Calories (kcal)	Total Time (min)
25	Mediterranean Breakfast Quinoa	7.9	53.9	11.5	327	25
26	Fresh Blackberries Quinoa	24.3	80.7	16.4	597	20
27	Quinoa Breakfast Bowl	26.8	24.1	12.7	372	25
28	Quinoa Hot Breakfast Cereal	8	40.8	7.9	257	15
29	Quinoa Muffins	4.5	7.8	5.6	94	35
30	Power Oatmeal	11.4	27.4	9.5	242	25
31	Blueberry and Banana Steel Cut Oats	5.7	76.8	7.6	385	15
32	Pumpkin Oatmeal	4.7	38.7	9.4	229	8
33	No-Cook Overnight Oatmeal	9.6	41.1	9.5	279	8 h
34	Hearty Apple Almond Oatmeal	31.9	67.6	18	594	10
35	Portobello Pesto Egg Omelette	12	12	28	259	25
36	Zucchini Egg White Frittata	5	7.9	16.5	137	25
37	Crustless Spinach Quiche	23.7	4.8	20.4	309	50
38	Spinach Salad with Warm Bacon-Mustard Dressing	40.6	40.1	36.1	663	20

Page	Meal	Fat (grams)	Carbs (grams)	Protein (grams)	Calories (kcal)	Total Time (min)
39	Asparagus Mushroom Bacon Crustless Quiche	25.9	3.9	11.5	291	55
40	Cucumber-Avocado Sandwich	32.5	46.3	11.4	496	10
41	Delicious Avocado Sandwich	24.2	34.4	19.9	428	10
42	Avocado and Orange Sandwich	23.7	42.6	12	407	10
43	Avocado Prosciutto Ham Sandwich	33.3	55.1	20.8	582	15
44	Lemon Avocado Toast	2.3	12.4	3.8	84	13
45	Hummus and Prosciutto Wrap	23.4	24	20	345	23
46	Black Bean and Couscous Salad	5.9	41.2	10.4	255	35
47	Almond Berry Smoothie	11.7	55.6	5.3	312	10
48	Raspberry Blackberry Smoothie	1.7	42.5	5.8	195	10
49	Banana Green Smoothie	0.8	77.4	18.6	367	5
50	Vegan Strawberry Oatmeal Smoothie	2.9	42.4	4.2	205	10

Lunch

Page	Meal	Fat (grams)	Carbs (grams)	Protein (grams)	Calories (kcal)	Total Time (min)
52	Effortless Tuna	15.5	13.9	31.3	325	25
53	Yummy Tuna	15.6	36.6	16.4	353	30
54	Salad Nicoise	8.7	34.7	17.5	287	2h 45min
55	Pleasurable Tuna	33	45.3	31.7	599	30
56	Spinach and Sardine Sandwich	23	29	21	409	10
57	Sardine and Potato Salad with Arugula	19.1	33.3	9.1	347	35
58	Pan-Fried Sardines	24	16	17	356	56
59	Hearty Salmon Quinoa Burgers	13	17	23	277	30
61	Salmon Crostini	4.3	16.7	8.2	347	16
62	Potato Baked Salmon	30.5	49.1	44.5	650	50
64	Chicken Tostados	8.8	23.3	32.6	307	55
65	Chicken Corn Salad	24	25	34	449	35
66	Chicken Fried Rice	2	21	18	179	25
67	Chicken and Pepper Fajitas	13	39	18	348	20
68	Chicken Salad with Grapes	25	15	22	360	31
69	Southwestern Chicken Salad	4	38	9	267	41
70	Tortilla Coated Chicken Tenders	11	22	34	331	25

Page	Meal	Fat (grams)	Carbs (grams)	Protein (grams)	Calories (kcal)	Total Time (min)
71	Chicken with Sesame Cucumber Relish	8	21	29	278	30
73	Stuffed Delicata Squash with Chicken	8	30.5	15	240	45
74	Corn and Chicken Salad with Salsa Dressing	15.5	17	25	288	15
75	Stuffed Turkey Breasts With Butternut Squash	8	25	22	258	1h 2min8
77	Turkey Lettuce Wraps	13	21	31	297	26
79	Leftover Turkey Tacos	5	30	21.5	235	15
80	Turkey Tortillas	7	54	22	366	50
81	Tacos with Turkey	9	39	21	390	1 hour
83	Pork and Asparagus	32	8	39	476	35
84	Boneless Pork Chops	9	9	28	230	35
86	Pork Skewers	4	0	11	91	20
87	Pork Tenderloin Apricot Salad	10	25	25	247	40
89	Pork Tenderloin with Blue Cheese	11.3	21	26	297	30

Dinner

Page	Meal	Fat (grams)	Carbs (grams)	Protein (grams)	Calories (kcal)	Total Time (min)
91	Appetizing Tuna	13.6	2	13.6	186	15
92	Avocado and Tuna	18.2	11	23.9	294	20
93	Cauliflower and Tuna	15	3	7	179	45
94	Grilled Salmon Kebabs One Way	11	7	35	267	20
95	Grilled Cedar Plank Salmon	11	8	30	251	30
97	Salmon Burgers With Sriracha Mayo	15	2.1	32.6	290	1h 30min
99	Arugula Salmon Salad	16.1	11	26	288	20
100	Tilapia With Peppers and Olives	13	8	35	276	20
101	Cilantro Tilapia	12.1	0.3	22.9	200.1	17
102	Tilapia Al Ajillo	13	1	34	257	20
103	Savory Lemon	12	1	21	197	21
104	Shrimp Skewers with Garlic-Lime Marinade	5	1	15	108	20
105	Grilled Salmon Kebobs Other Way	22	2	24	308	33
106	Lemon Pepper Salmon Caesar Salad	22	7	25	323	40
108	Chicken Breasts with Mushroom	16	8	35	315	40

Page	Meal	Fat (grams)	Carbs (grams)	Protein (grams)	Calories (kcal)	Total Time (min)
110	Chicken and Tomato Salad	19	10	17	278	40
112	Chicken with Lemon	4	1	25	179	45
113	Chicken Rollatini	14	10	25	267	35
115	Chicken with Olives and Herbs	11	4.5	52.5	351	26
116	Chicken and Veggie Dinner	20	15.5	46.5	429	45
118	Superb Chicken Salad	8	13	29	245	308
120	Breaded Chicken Cutlets	13	12	31	286	30
122	Chicken And Tomato Kebabs	7.5	3	18	147	3h 6min
123	Chicken With Garlic Yogurt Sauce	11	5	30	240	1h 15min
125	Greek Feta-Zucchini Turkey Burgers	11	10	20	221	30

Snack

Page	Meal	Fat (grams)	Carbs (grams)	Protein (grams)	Calories (kcal)	Total Time (min)
128	Crispy Lentil Energy Bites	6.2	22.6	5.8	162	1h 10min
129	Zesty Black Bean Hummus	7.5	20	16	218	5
130	Roasted Chickpeas	8.5	60.5	20.5	395	55
131	Portobello Mushroom Delight	8.5	2	8.5	122	20
132	Greek Peanut Butter Yogurt	17.1	22.4	27.9	359	5
133	Tuna Salad on Crackers	7	9	13	393	10
134	Hardboiled Egg and Avocado Bowl	17.6	8	13.4	246	17
135	Chipotle Lime Edamame	15	16	16	232	10
136	Mediterranean Picnic Snack	9	22	7	197	5
137	Tomato-Basil Skewers	3	1	3	46	10

Dessert

Page	Meal	Fat (grams)	Carbs (grams)	Protein (grams)	Calories (kcal)	Total Time (min)
139	Greek Baklava	25.9	37.5	6.1	393	1h 5min
140	Pumpkin Pie Smoothie	0.8	18.6	2.6	84	5
141	Key Lime Pie	1.4	7.1	0.9	42.6	2h 5min
142	Chocolate Cupcakes	4.5	22.3	1.9	127.7	45
143	Easy Tasty Frozen Pie	0.7	1	0.7	13.1	5
144	Ice Cream Sandwich	1.4	5.8	0.6	37.3	1
145	Caramel Apple Fluff	0.1	13.6	0.3	51.5	2h 5min
146	Pumpkin Cupcakes	3	17.5	1.1	100.2	35
147	Pink Fluff	1	11.8	0.7	50.3	1 hour
148	Yogurt Fluff	0.1	4.8	3.5	50.3	35

Bake Chicken Breasts in the Oven

Prep time: 10 min / Cook time: 40 min / Total Time: 50 min

Ingredients:

Extra-virgin olive oil

1 or more boneless, skinless chicken breasts

Salt and pepper

Other spices or seasonings

Equipment:

Baking dish

Parchment paper

Instant-read thermometer

Directions:

1   Preheat the oven to 400 degrees Fahrenheit with a rack in the middle position. Using the olive oil, rub the pan and one side of the parchment paper, this will prevent the chicken from sticking.

2   Pat the chicken dry and rub on a little olive oil, if desired. Sprinkle with salt and pepper, and any other seasonings of your liking.

3   In the baking dish place the chicken breasts, arranged slightly apart. For the extra flavor, you can also tuck herbs or lemon wedges around.

4   Over the chicken lay the parchment paper, butter-side down.

5   Cover the chicken with parchment paper, butter-side down. Tuck the edges into the pan and press the parchment paper down so that it's snug neatly around the chicken. Parchment paper should completely cover chicken breasts.

6   Place the chicken in the oven and bake until the chicken is completely opaque all the way through and an instant-read thermometer registers 165 degrees Fahrenheit. Begin checking after 20 minutes, total cooking time is usually around 30 – 40 minutes.

7   Serve the chicken immediately, or let it cool down and refrigerate for up to a week. *Enjoy!*

Cook Chicken Breasts in the Pan

Prep time: 10 min / Cook time: 21 min / Total Time: 31 min

Ingredients:

1 tbsp. extra-virgin olive oil	Salt and pepper
1 or more boneless, skinless chicken breasts	Other spices or seasonings

Equipment:

Meat tenderizer	Tongs or spatula
Wide (10-inch) sauté pan with lid	Instant-read thermometer

Directions:

1   Use meat tenderizer to pound the chicken breast to an even thickness.

2   Lightly salt and pepper the chicken breasts.

3   Over medium-high heat place the sauté pan and add the olive oil when the pan gets quite hot. Softly swirl the pan to cover the pan with the olive oil.

4   Lower the heat to medium. Add the chicken breasts. Cook for about 1 minute to help them get that slightly golden color on one side (you are not actually searing or browning them).

5   Turn each chicken breast over and lower the heat to low.

6   Cover the pan with a tight-fitting lid, set a timer for 10 minutes, and leave them be. Do not peek by lifting the lid. Just let them be.

7   After the 10 minutes have passed, turn off the heat. (Remove the pan from the heat source if you have an electric stove). Reset the timer for another 10 minutes and leave the chicken breasts be in the pan. Again, just let them be, do not peek.

8   After the 10 minutes have passed, take off the lid, and your chicken breasts are done.

9   To make sure they are done, please, just check that there is no pink color in the middle of the chicken breasts. You can use an instant-read thermometer to check, if you want to be absolutely sure it is cooked (the middle of the chicken should be at least 165 degrees Fahrenheit. Slice the chicken breasts and eat. *Enjoy!*

Cook Turkey Breast in the Oven

Prep time: 15 min / Cook time: 2 hours / Total Time: 2 hours 15 min

Ingredients:

3 to 7 lbs. thawed, bone-in, skin-on turkey breast (1 half-breast or 1 whole turkey breast joined at the breast bone)

1 tablespoon extra-virgin olive oil

1 tablespoon kosher salt

1/2 tsp. black pepper

Equipment:

Roasting pan, oven-proof skillet, or other baking dish large enough to hold the whole breast

Roasting rack, or thick-cut vegetables to lift the breast off the pan

Measuring spoons

Aluminum foil

Directions:

1   Place the turkey breast on top of vegetables in a skillet, or transfer the turkey breast to the rack inside a roasting pan, or other baking dish.

2   Put an oven rack in the bottom third of the oven. Preheat the oven to 450 degrees Fahrenheit.

3   With the use of a paper towel pat the skin dry of the turkey breast. Rub the turkey breast with the olive oil. Sprinkle the breast with salt and pepper. Rub the seasonings into the skin.

4   Transfer the turkey in the oven and immediately turn the heat down to 350 degrees Fahrenheit. Roast for 1 hour, then start checking the temperature. Continue checking every 10 – 15 minutes till the breast is cooked through.

5   When the temperature reaches 165 degrees Fahrenheit in the thickest part of the breast meat, the turkey is done.

6   Cover the turkey breast with aluminum foil to prevent scorching if the skin begins to brown too darkly toward the end of cooking

7   When cooked, take out the turkey from the oven and cover it with foil, loosely. To give the juices time to redistribute rest the turkey for 15 – 20 minutes.

8   Carve the turkey starting at the breast bone. Continue carving, placing your knife as close to the ribs as possible, till the entire breast is carved from the bone. Slice the breast crosswise into slices. *Enjoy!*

Cook Salmon in the Oven

Prep time: 10 min / Cook time: 21 min / Total Time: 31 min

Ingredients:

1 or more (6-ounce) salmon fillets

Extra-virgin olive oil

Salt

Pepper

Lemon wedges, to serve

Equipment:

Roasting pan or baking sheet

Aluminum foil

Directions:

1   With a rack placed in the middle preheat the oven to a 425 degrees Fahrenheit. Line a baking sheet or a roasting pan with a foil.

2   With a paper towel pat the salmon dry.

3   Over the top of each salmon drizzle some olive oil (just enough to coat the salmon) and with your fingers or a pastry brush rub it over the salmon. Generously sprinkle the salmon with salt and pepper.

4   Transfer the salmon into the roasting pan, skin side down and place it into the preheated oven.

5   Roasting time will depend on the thickness of the salmon. For every half-inch of salmon, roast 4 – 6 minutes.

6   You can use the fork to check the doneness of your salmon. It's ready when the salmon flakes easily with a fork.

7   You can also use an instant-read thermometer to check the salmon for doneness. The thickest part of the salmon fillet should read the internal temperature of around 145 degrees Fahrenheit. *Enjoy!*

Cook Pan-Seared Salmon

Prep time: 5 min / Cook time: 10 min / Total Time: 15 min

Ingredients:

1 or more (6-ounce) salmon fillets	Salt
1 tablespoon extra-virgin olive oil	Pepper

Equipment:

Paper towels or dish towel	Fish spatula
Skillet or frying pan	Medium plate
Measuring spoon	

Directions:

1   To give your salmon enough time to come to room temperature remove it from the refrigerator about 15 minutes before you're ready to cook.

2   Pat each fillet dry, both on top and bottom, by using a clean dish towel or a paper towel, to prevent fillets from sticking to the pan.

3   Place on the stovetop over a medium-high heat stainless steel or cast iron skillet. Let the pan heat up for a couple of minutes.

4   Once the pan is hot enough (you can test it by flicking few drops of water into the pan to see if it evaporates almost immediately, the pan is ready to go) add 1 tablespoon of olive oil to the pan. Coat the bottom with a thin layer of olive oil by tilting the skillet. Heat the olive oil in the skillet till you see ripples across the surface, but not that long that it starts to smoke.

5   Season the fillets with salt and pepper just before adding them to the skillet.

6   Add them to the skillet, carefully, one at a time, skin-side down.

7   The salmon will be cooking the majority of time skin-side down in the pan. It's important that you do not poke, prod, or move the fish. Just leave it be. Ass the fillets are cooking, you'll notice that the color is beginning to lighten, starting from the bottom side near the skin and slowly moving up.

8   Flip the fish when the lighter-colored flesh has moved about 3/4 of the way up the fillets. When turning flip the fish away from you to prevent any oil splatter.

9   Cook for an extra 2 minutes for a thicker fillets and 1- 2 minutes for thinner fillets.

10   By using a fish spatula remove the fillets from the pan and place them, skin-side down, on a paper towel-lined plate.

11   Let them cool down for about 3 minutes before serving. *Enjoy!*

YOUR ULTIMATE GROCERY LIST

Gluten-FREE Foods

This list contains foods that are naturally gluten free when unprocessed. But always check the label on items with more than one ingredient.

GLUTEN FREE					CONTAINS GLUTEN
MEAT	**VEGETABLES**	**FRUIT**	**DAIRY**	**GRAINS/ FLOURS**	**DERIVED FROM GLUTEN**
BEEF	All Dry Beans	Apples	Butter	Almond Flour	Barley
Chuck Roast	Artichokes	Apricots		Amaranth	Rye
Ground Beef*	Arugula	Bananas	**CHEESE**	Arrowroot	Malt
(Check Beef Burgers)	Asparagus	Blackberries	American	Brown Rice	Malt Vinegar
	Avocado	Blueberries	Cheddar	Brown rice flour	Triticale
Ribs	Beets	Cantaloupe	Cottage Cheese	Buckwheat	Wheat
Steak	Bell Peppers	Cherries	Cream Cheese	Coconut flour	Durum
	Black Eyed Peas	Cranberries	Monterrey Jack	Corn Flour	Graham
Buffalo	Brocolli	Currents	Parmesan	Corn Grits	Semolina
	Brussels Sprouts	Dates	Pepper Jack	Corn Meal*	Kamut
All fish	Cabbage	Figs	Romano	Flaxseed	Spelt
	Carrots	Grapes	Swiss	Manioc	
POULTRY	Cauliflower	Guava	Cream	Millet	**PRODUCTS CONTAINING**
Chicken Breasts	Celery	Honey Dew Melon	Eggs	Oats**	
Chicken Legs	Corn	Kiwi	Half and Half	Potato flour	
Duck	Cucumber	Kumquat	Ice Cream*	Quinoa	Breading
Goose	Egg Plant	Lemons	Milk	Rice flour	Borth, (Soup, Bases)

| GLUTEN FREE | | | | | CONTAINS GLUTEN |
MEAT	VEGETABLES	FRUIT	DAIRY	GRAINS/ FLOURS	DERIVED FROM GLUTEN
Lamb	Garlic	Limes	Sour Cream	Tapioca Flour	Brown Rice Syrup
Veal	Green Beans	Mangos	Yogurt	Taro Flour	Candy/Sweets *
Venison	Kale	Oranges		White Rice	Croutons
Whole Chicken	Lettuce	Papaya	bluecheese is		Flour or Cereal Products
Whole Turkey	Mushrooms	Passion Fruit	NOT gluten free!		Immitation Bacon/Seafood
	Okra	Peaches			Marinades
PORK	Onions	Pears			Pastas
Ham* (Glaze)	Pumpkin				Sauces, Gravies
Pepperoni	Radish				Soy Sauce
Pork Chops	Red Potato				Stuffing
Pork Ribs	Romaine Lettuce				Thickeners
	Russet Potato				Communion Wafers
LUNCHMEAT*	Tomatoes				Many Over-The-Counter Drugs
Ham	Squash				
Turkey	Watercress				
Roast Beef	Zucchini				* Except Liquorice
Salami					

*Starred items require special attention to labels because gluten tends to be added to them.

Fiber-RICH Foods

FOOD ITEM	AMOUNT	TOTAL FIBRE (g)	SOLUBLE FIBRE (g)	INSOLUBLE FIBRE (g)
VEGETABLES, (Cooked)				
Asparagus	½ cup	2,8	1,7	1,1
Beets, (Flesh only)	½ cup	1,8	1,8	1
Broccoli	½ cup	2,4	1,2	1,2
Brussels Sprouts	½ cup	3,8	2	1,8
Carrots, (Sliced)	½ cup	2	1,1	0,9
Cauliflower	½ cup	1	0,4	0,6
Kale	½ cup	2,5	0,7	1,8
Okra, (Frozen)	½ cup	4,1	1	3,1
Peas, (Green, Frozen)	½ cup	4,3	1,3	3
Spinach	½ cup	1,6	0,5	1,1
Turnip	½ cup	4,8	1,7	3,1
FRUITS				
Apple, (Red, Fresh with skin	1 small	2,8	1	1,8
Apricots, (Dried)	7 halves	2	1,1	0,9
Banana, (Fresh)	½ small	1,1	0,3	0,8
Blueberries, (Fresh)	¾ cup	1,4	0,3	1,1
Mango, (Fresh, Flesh only)	½ small	2,9	1,7	1,2
Pear, (Fresh, With skin)	½ large	2,9	1,1	1,8
Raspberries, (Fresh)	1 cup	3,3	0,9	2,4
Strawberries, (Fresh)	1 ¼ cup	2,8	1,1	1,7
LEGUMES (Cooked)				
Black Beans	½ cup	6,1	2,4	3,7
Kidney Beans, (Light red)	½ cup	7,9	2	5,9
Lentils	½ cup	5,2	0,6	4,6
Lima Beans	½ cup	4,3	1,1	3,2
Pinto Beans	½ cup	6,1	1,4	4,7
PASTAS, BREADS & GRAINS				
Popcorn, (Popped)	3 cups	2	0,1	1,9
Rice, (White, Cooked)	½ cup	0,8	trace	0,8

FOOD ITEM	AMOUNT	TOTAL FIBRE (g)	SOLUBLE FIBRE (g)	INSOLUBLE FIBRE (g)
Spaghetti, (Whole wheat, Cooked)	½ cup	2,7	0,6	2,1
Wheat Bran	½ cup	12,3	1	11,3
Pumpernickel Bread	1 slice	2,7	1,2	1,5
Whole Wheat Bread	1 slice	1,5	0,3	1,2
CEREALS				
Oatmeal, (Dry)	1/3 cup	2,7	1,4	1,3
Shredded Wheat	1 cup	5,2	0,7	4,5
All Bran	1/3 cup	8,6	1,4	7,2
Fiber One	½ cup	11,9	0,8	11,1
Oat Flakes	1 cup	3,1	1,5	1,6
NUTS & SEEDS				
Almonds	6 whole	0,6	0,1	0,5
Flaxseeds	1 tbsp	3,3	1,1	2,2
Peanut Butter, (Smooth)	1 tbsp	1	0,3	0,7
Peanuts, (Roasted)	10 large	0,6	0,2	0,4
Sesame Seeds	1 tbsp	0,5	0,2	0,3
Sunflower Seeds	1 tbsp	0,5	0,2	0,3
Walnuts	2 whole	0,3	0,1	0,2

Nutritional Values

(per 100g, Uncooked, Ordered A-Z per Category)	Calories	Protein	Carbs	Fats
FOOD ITEMS				
PROTEIN				
BEEF (Per 100g, uncooked)	Calories	Protein	Carbs	Fats
Beef (95% Lean Ground Beef)	137	21	0	5
Beef (Bottom Round Roast)	187	27	0	8
Beef (Brisket, Flat Half)	213	33	0	8
Beef (Eye Round Roast)	168	29	0	5
Beef (Flank Steak)	192	28	0	8
Beef (Mock Tender Steak)	160	26	0	6
Beef (New York Steak)	193	29	0	8
Beef (Rib Eye Steak)	274	18	0	22
Beef (Round Tip Roast)	188	27	0	8
Beef (Shoulder Steak)	182	26	0	8
Beef (T-Bone)	220	19	0	15
Beef (Tenderloin)	218	28	0	18
Beef (Top Round Steak)	209	36	0	6
Beef (Top Sirloin Steak)	212	29	0	10
Beef (Tri Tip)	142	21	0	6
POULTRY (Per 100g, uncooked)	Calories	Protein	Carbs	Fats
Chicken (Breast, Skin Removed)	114	21	0	2,5
Chicken (Liver)	116	17	0	5
Chicken (Thigh, Skin Removed)	126	19	0	5
Duck (Breast, Skin Removed)	132	18	0	6
Egg (Protein Powder)	357	78,6	7,1	0

(per 100g, Uncooked, Ordered A-Z per Category)	Calories	Protein	Carbs	Fats
FOOD ITEMS				
Egg (Whites, Hard boiled, No Yolk)	36	9	0	0
Egg (Whites, 1 large egg white is 33g)	48	11	0,7	0,2
Egg (Whole, 1 large egg white is 50g)	155	13	1,1	11
Goose (Breast, Skin Removed)	161	23	0	7
Turkey (Ground, 99% Fat Free)	112	23	0	1,8
Turkey (Breast, Skin Removed)	115	24	0	2
OTHER MEAT (Per 100g, uncooked)	Calories	Protein	Carbs	Fats
Bacon (Cured)	458	12	1	45
Bison (Grass fed)	146	20	0	7
Buffalo (Ground)	99	20	0	1
Ham (Cured)	195	28	0	8
Lamb (Chop)	208	18	0	14
Lamb (Leg)	195	19	0	13
Pork (Chop)	123	21	0	4
Pork (Ribs)	152	22	0	6
Rabbit	114	22	0	2
Veal	112	20	0	3
Venison	157	22	0	7
FISH (Per 100g, uncooked)	Calories	Protein	Carbs	Fats
Cod	82	18	0	0,7
Haddock	87	19	0	1
Halibut	110	21	0	2
Rainbow Trout	150	23	0	6

(per 100g, Uncooked, Ordered A-Z per Category)	Calories	Protein	Carbs	Fats
FOOD ITEMS				
Salmon	180	20,2	0	11
Sardines	160	17	0	9
Sole Fillet	80	17	0	1,5
Tuna (Tinned Brine)	99	23,5	0	0,6
Tuna (Steak)	144	23,3	0	4,9
Tuna (Albacore, Tinned, No Added Salt)	130	27,8	0	2,8
DAIRY (Per 100g, uncooked)	Calories	Protein	Carbs	Fats
Cheese (Cheddar)	113	7	0,4	9,3
Cheese (Cream)	297	6,7	2,6	29,7
Cheese (Feta)	263	14	4	21
Cottage Cheese (Lowfat, 1% Milkfat)	72	12	2,7	1
Ice Cream (Vanilla, Fat free)	138	4	30	0
Milk (Lowfat, 1% Milkfat)	42	3,4	5	1
Sour Cream (Cultured)	217	3,3	4,1	20,9
Yogurt (Plain, Goats Milk)	70	2,35	5,3	4
Yogurt (FAGE 2%)	130	17	8	4

CARBOHYDRATES

GRAINS, STARCHES & CEREALS (Per 100g, uncooked)	Calories	Protein	Carbs	Fats
Bran Fiber	216	16	65	4
Bran Flakes	320	9,3	80	2,31
Buckwheat	335	13	71	3
Couscous	376	13	77	1
Granola	489	15	53	24

Museli (Swiss Style)	364	11	61	6,4
Oats	356	11	60	8
Oats (Gluten Free, Rolled)	389	17	66	7
Pasta (Macaroni, Whole-wheat)	348	15	75	1
Pasta (Spaghetti, Whole-wheat)	347	14,5	75	1,4
Potato (Sweet)	90	2	21	0
Potato (Yam)	118	1,5	28	0,2
Potatos (Baby)	66	1,4	15,4	0,3
Quinoa	368	14	64	6
Rice (Brown, Medium-Grain)	362	8	76	3
Rice (White, Medium-Grain)	360	7	79	1
Rice Cake	372	8	78,7	2,8
Shredded Wheat	347	12	81	0
Wheat Germ (Raw, Uncooked)	333	20	67	3,3
Wheetabix (2 Biscuits = 35g)	334	10	66	0
Baby Potatos	66	1,4	15,4	0,3
BAKED (Per 100g, uncooked)	Calories	Protein	Carbs	Fats
Bagel, Cinnamon-raisin	273	10	55	2
Bread (Flax Seed)	255	11	47	6
Bread (Rye)	190	6	35	2
Bread, (White, Low sodium, 1 slice 25g)	267	8	50	4
Bread, (Whole-wheat, 1 slice 28g)	247	13	41	3
Muffin, (English, Plain, Enriched)	235	8	46	2
Muffin, Blueberry (1 small 71g)	255	4	50	4
Pitta, (White, Enriched, 1 large 60g)	165	5	33	1
Pitta, (Whole-wheat, 1 large 64g)	266	10	55	3

VEGETABLES & BEANS (Per 100g, uncooked)	Calories	Protein	Carbs	Fats
Alfalfa Seeds	23	4	2	1
Arugula	25	3	4	1
Asparagus	26	3,4	1,4	0,8
Avocado	160	2	9	15
Beets	43	2	10	0
Bok Choy	17	1,2	3,2	0,2
Broccoli	34	2,8	7	0,4
Brussels Sprouts	43	3	9	0
Cabbage	26	4	1	0
Red Cabbage	31	1,4	7	0,2
Carrots	24	0,6	4,9	0,4
Cauliflower	25	1,9	5	0,3
Celery	7	0,5	0,9	0,2
Chickpeas	164	9	27	3
Corn (Yellow)	86	3	19	1
Courgette/Zuchinni	19	2	2	0,4
Cucumber	15	1	4	0
Egg Plant/Aubergine	15	0	2	15
Garlic	149	6	33	0
Green Beans	31	1,8	7	0,2
Kale	49	4,3	9	0,9
Kidney Beans	84	5	16	1
Lettuce	14	0,8	1,7	0,5
Mange Tout	26	3,2	3,3	0,1
Mixed Baby Greens	18	2,4	4,7	0
Mushroom (Portabello)	35	4	5	1
Mushroom (White)	22	3,1	3,3	0,3

Okra	31	2	7	0
Onion	40	1	9	0
Peas (Frozen, Boiled)	69	6	9,7	0,9
Potato (Red)	70	2	16	0
Potato (White)	77	2	18	0
Pumkin	26	1	6	0
Radish	16	1	3	0
Red Bell Pepper	31	1	6	0,2
Spaghetti Squash	31	0,6	7	0,6
Spinach	23	2,9	3,6	0,4
Spring Onion	32	1,8	7,3	0,2
Squash	16	1	3	0
Tomato (Red)	19	1	4	0
White Kidney Beans	84	5	15	0,5
FRUIT (Per 100g, uncooked)	Calories	Protein	Carbs	Fats
Apple	48	0	13	0
Apricots	29	0,8	6,6	0,1
Banana	89	1	23	0
Blackberries	43	1	10	0
Blueberries	57	1	14	0
Cherries	63	1	16	0
Cranberries	46	0	12	0
Dates	277	2	75	5
Figs	74	1	19	0
Grapes	67	1	17	0
Kiwi	61	1	15	1
Lemon	29	1	9	0
Lime	30	1	11	0
Mango	65	1	17	0

Melon (Honeydew)	36	1	9	0
Melon (Watermelon)	30	1	8	0
Orange	46	1	12	0
Peaches	39	1	10	0
Pears	36	0,3	9,1	0,1
Pineapple	50	1	13	0,1
Rasins	299	3	79	0
Raspberries	53	1,2	12	0,6
Strawberries	32	0,7	7,7	0,3

NON-FRUIT/VEGETABLE (Per 100g, uncooked)	Calories	Protein	Carbs	Fats
Almond Milk (Original)	70	2	10	2,5
Apple Sauce	49	0	12	0
Raw Honey	304	0,3	82	0
Soy Milk (Original)	43	3	5	1

FATS				
NUTS, SEEDS & OILS (Per 100g, uncooked)	Calories	Protein	Carbs	Fats
Alfalfa Seed	402	44	44	5,6
Almond Butter	703	17,8	21,4	60,7
Almonds (Shelled, Raw)	603	21,1	4,2	55,8
Bragg Ginger & Sesame	387	0	6,7	40
Cacao Nibs (Organic, Raw)	580	14,3	43	39
Cashew (Raw)	577	17,7	18,1	48,2
Coconut Oil	900	0	0	100
Flax Seed (Golden Roasted)	611	20	27	47
Flaxseed Oil	900	0	0	100

Macadmia Oil (1Tbsp)	126	0	0	14
MCT Oil	840	0	0	93,3
Olive Oil (Unrefined, Cold-Pressed)	900	0	0	100
Olives (Pitted, Ripe, Canned)	175	0	6,6	16,5
Peanut Butter (Organic)	623	28	22	47
Pine Nuts	720	14	13	68
Pumpkin Seeds	288	25	17,85	13
Sunflower oil	899	0	0	99,9
Sunflower Seeds	607	21,42	17,85	50
UDO's Oil	876	1,3	0	96,8
Tahini	638	17	21	54

CONCLUSION

Thank you again for investing in my cookbook!

I hope this book was able to help you to prepare your weight loss meal plans and learn how to cook easy Mediterranean dishes.

The next step is to start stocking up on healthy ingredients and turn your kitchen into a Mediterranean diet heaven.

One last thing.

Can I ask you for a small favor?

> If you don't like writing reviews that much,
> please think of me next time when you do.

If you do decide to leave me a review on Amazon YOU will be helping other buyers, just like you, in making better-informed buying decision.

I do read all the reviews personally to hear my readers so I can better grow as a writer and serve you, my reader, with books that can change your life for the better.

APPENDIX

A - The Dirty Dozen & the Clean Fifteen: Choose Organic

A nonprofit and environmental watchdog institution called Environmental Working Group (EWG) reviews the data provided by the US Department of Agriculture (USDA) and the Food and Drug Administration (FDA) about pesticide residues and assembles a list each year of the best and worst pesticide loads discovered in commercial crops.

You can use these lists to choose which fruits and vegetables to buy organic to reduce your exposure to pesticides and which produce is regarded safe enough to skip the organics. This does not mean they are pesticide-free, so wash these fruits and vegetables carefully. These lists adjust every year, so make sure you look up the most current before you fill your shopping cart. You'll discover the most recent lists as well as a guide to pesticides in produce at EWG.org/ FoodNews.

2019 DIRTY DOZEN	2019 CLEAN FIFTEEN
Strawberries	Avocados
Spinach	Sweet Corn
Kale	Pineapples
Nectarines	Frozen sweet peas
Apples	Onions
Grapes	Papayas
Peaches	Eggplants
Cherries	Asparagus
Pears	Kiwis
Tomatoes	Cabbages
Celery	Cauliflower
Potatoes	Cantaloupes
	Broccoli
	Mushrooms
	Honeydew melons

B - Conversion Tables

Volume Equivalents (Dry)

American Standard	Metric
1/8 tsp.	.5 ml
1/4 tsp.	1 ml
1/2 tsp.	2 ml
3/4 tsp.	4 ml
1 tsp.	5 ml
1 tablespoon	15 ml
1/4 cup	59 ml

American Standard	Metric
1/3 cup	79 ml
1/2 cup	118 ml
2/3 cup	158 ml
3/4 cup	177 ml
1 cup	225 ml
2 cups or 1 pint	450 ml
3 cups	675 ml
4 cups or 1 quart	1 liter
1/2 gallon	2 liters
1 gallon	4 liters

Volume Equivalents (Liquid)

American Standard (Cups & Quarts)	American Standard (Ounces)	Metric (Milliliters & Liters)
2 tbsp.	1 fl. oz.	30 ml
1/4 cup	2 fl. oz.	60 ml
1/2 cup	4 fl. oz.	125 ml
1 cup	8 fl. oz.	250 ml
1 1/2 cup	12 fl. oz.	375 ml
2 cups or 1 pint	16 fl. oz.	500 ml
4 cups or 1 quart	32 fl. oz.	1000 ml or 1 liter
1 gallon	128 fl. oz.	4 liters

Oven Temperatures Equivalents

American Standard	Metric
250° F	130° C
300° F	150° C
350° F	180° C
400° F	200° C
450° F	230° C

Weight Equivalents (Mass)

American Standard (Ounces)	Metric (Grams)
1/2 ounce	15 grams
1 ounce	30 grams
3 ounces	85 grams
3.75 ounces	100 grams
4 ounces	115 grams
8 ounces	225 grams
12 ounces	340 grams
16 ounces or 1 lbs.	450 grams

Printed in Great Britain
by Amazon

27037871R00112